MAHATMA GANDHI – Th

PORBANDAR, GUJARAT — ITS BEACHES CARESSED BY THE WAVES OF THE ARABIAN SEA.

IT WAS ABOUT THE 1820s. KHIMOJI, RANA OF PORBANDAR, WAS TALKING TO HIS PRIME MINISTER.

SURELY, UTTAMCHAND, THERE IS NO DIWAN AS CAPABLE AS YOU.

YOU ARE BEING KIND, RANAJI.

THE PRAISE WAS WELL DESERVED, FOR UTTAMCHAND SERVED HIS RULER DEVOTEDLY.

BUT, AFTER THE RANA'S DEATH, UTTAMCHAND DID NOT RECEIVE THE SAME TREATMENT FROM THE SUCCESSOR, AND HE FELT UNHAPPY.

LAKSHMI, WE CAN NO LONGER STAY HERE. LET US GO TO OUR ANCESTRAL HOME AT KUTIYANA*.

LATER, INVITED BY THE NAWAB OF JUNAGADH, UTTAMCHAND WENT TO HIS COURT TO PAY HIS RESPECTS. HE SALUTED THE NAWAB WITH HIS LEFT HAND.

UTTAMCHAND, WHY THIS DISCOURTESY TO THE NAWAB SAHEB?

SIRE, MY RIGHT HAND IS ALREADY PLEDGED TO PORBANDAR.

BRAVO, UTTAMCHAND. I WOULD GIVE HALF MY KINGDOM TO HAVE A DIWAN LIKE YOU.

THANK YOU, SIRE, BUT I HAVE NO WISH TO SERVE ANY MORE.

SUCH WAS THE TRUTHFULNESS, SENSE OF LOYALTY AND COURAGE OF UTTAMCHAND. HE WAS THE GRANDFATHER OF MOHANDAS GANDHI.

* IN JUNAGADH STATE

1

RAJKOT. THE 1870s. THAKORE BAVAJIRAJ WAS ENJOYING HIMSELF.

THIS IS FINE WINE. THE FINEST I'VE TASTED! HA, HA, HA!

JUST THEN—

THAKORE SAHIB! YOUR DIWAN IS HERE TO SEE YOU.

OH, NO! QUICK, TAKE AWAY THESE GLASSES...

YOU, THERE! OPEN THE WINDOWS. LET THE SMELLS ESCAPE...

THAKORE SAHIB!

HE, HE, HE. COME IN, KARAM-CHAND. I WAS... ER... GOING THROUGH THESE IMPORTANT PAPERS...

HMM!... HOW OFTEN I HAVE TOLD YOU THIS. DO NOT LIVE A WASTEFUL LIFE.

WASTEFUL LIFE? ME? OH, REALLY, KARAMCHAND...!

IF A RULER COULD BE IN SUCH AWE OF HIS MINISTER, WHAT KIND OF MAN WAS THIS MINISTER? THE SOUL OF HONESTY! HE WAS THE FATHER OF MOHANDAS GANDHI.

MOHANDAS KARAMCHAND GANDHI WAS BORN IN A THREE-STOREY HOUSE ON THE OUTSKIRTS OF PORBANDAR. KARAMCHAND WAS DIWAN OF PORBANDAR FOR MANY YEARS, AND LATER HE WENT OVER TO RAJKOT. MOHAN'S MOTHER WAS PUTALIBA.

ONE RAINY SEASON—

AND PUTALIBA CHEERFULLY CONTINUED TO FAST.

MOHAN AND HIS BROTHER, KARSAN, LOVED TO ROAM ABOUT IN THE NEIGHBOURHOOD AND CLIMB UP TREES.

* MOTHER

* THE KING WHO SOLD HIMSELF, HIS WIFE AND SON INTO SLAVERY FOR THE SAKE OF TRUTH.

YET, MOHAN SAW MANY FLAWS IN THE OTHERWISE RICH TRADITION THAT SURROUNDED HIM.

MONIYA, I JUST NOW SAW YOU TOUCHING UKA. HOW COULD YOU? HE CLEANS OUR LATRINES.

BUT, BA, WHAT'S THE DIFFERENCE BETWEEN UKA AND ME? IF GOD IS IN ALL THE WATER AND IN ALL THE LAND,⊕ HE IS IN UKA TOO...

... AN ANSWER THAT MUST HAVE GREATLY SURPRISED PUTALIBA.

MOHAN'S KIND AND GENTLE NATURE MADE HIM HIS MOTHER'S PET, BUT SHE WAS STRICT WITH HIM ABOUT CERTAIN THINGS.

MONIYA, IT'S TIME FOR SCHOOL. HURRY!

I'M COMING, BA.

BUT FOOD IS NOT READY YET.

NEVER MIND, RAMBHA. GIVE ME MY USUAL CURDS, KHAKHRA# AND... UM... SWEET AND SOUR MANGO PICKLE...

MANU, WHAT IS THIS? YOU MUST EAT PROPER MEALS.

I'LL BE LATE, BAPU.

TAKE THE HORSE AND CARRIAGE, THEN.

I'D RATHER WALK! THESE ARE MY HORSE AND CARRIAGE.

SOON AFTER, MOHAN JOINED THE ALFRED HIGH SCHOOL AT RAJKOT WHERE KARAMCHAND HAD TAKEN UP THE POST OF DIWAN.

BOYS, THE EDUCATION INSPECTOR, MR. GILES, IS COMING TODAY. BE SURE TO MAKE A GOOD IMPRESSION.

THE INSPECTOR GAVE THE BOYS FIVE WORDS AS A SPELLING EXERCISE. WHEN THE TEACHER STOPPED TO LOOK OVER MOHAN'S SHOULDER —

?

MOHAN HAD SPELT THE WORD 'KETTLE' WRONG.

⊕ 'JALE VISHNUH, STHALE VISHNUH' — A VERSE FROM THE VISHNU POOJA, OFTEN CHANTED IN THE GANDHI HOUSEHOLD. # UNLEAVENED BREAD ROUNDS BAKED CRISP.

THE TEACHER NUDGED MOHAN'S HEEL WITH THE POINT OF HIS BOOT TO DRAW HIS ATTENTION TO THE SPELLING MISTAKE.

BUT HONEST MOHAN DIDN'T UNDERSTAND THE HINT.

LATER—

MOHANDAS, YOU ARE THE ONLY BOY WHO SPELT A WORD WRONG. AND I SIGNALLED TO YOU TO... WELL, I DON'T UNDERSTAND YOUR STUPIDITY!

BY THIS 'STUPIDITY' A 12-YEAR-OLD WAS ALREADY READYING HIMSELF FOR A GREAT FUTURE IDEAL.

A DREAM TOO WAS FORMING IN THE BOY. WHEN KARAMCHAND ATTENDED THE STATE DURBARS HE HAD TO PUT ON OUTLANDISH STOCKINGS AND BOOTS.

OH, GOD! HOW I HATE THESE... HOW I HATE TO WEAR THEM!

THE BRITISH WANT TO BREAK OUR PRIDE BY SENSELESSLY MAKING US WEAR THEIR KIND OF CLOTHES. WE MUST FREE INDIA OF THEM.

AND AT MOHAN'S SCHOOL, HIS CLASSMATES OFTEN CHANTED A POEM.

THE ENGLISH RULE AND THE INDIANS MEEKLY SUBMIT... FOR LOOK AT THE DIFFERENCE IN THEIR BODILY STRENGTH, THE ENGLISHMAN IS FULL FIVE CUBITS TALL AND IS A MATCH FOR FIVE HUNDRED INDIANS.

IF ALL INDIANS ATE MEAT LIKE THE ENGLISH, MOHAN, WE'D BE ABLE TO CHASE OUT THE ENGLISH.

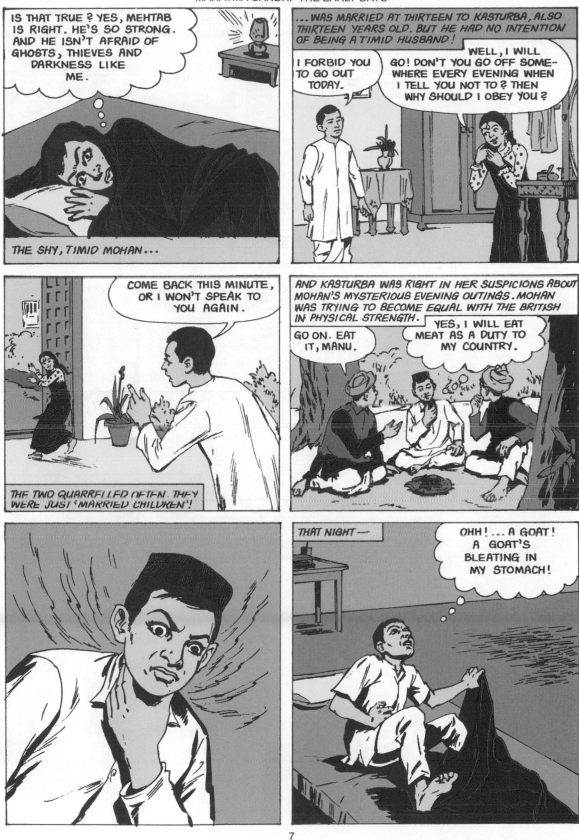

BUT MOHAN STUCK TO HIS 'DUTY' FOR A YEAR, TILL —

MONIYA, YOU HAVEN'T TOUCHED YOUR DINNER AGAIN TODAY. DID YOU EAT SOMETHING IN BETWEEN?

YES... I MEAN, NO. I...I JUST DON'T FEEL LIKE EATING.

I CAN'T BEAR IT ANYMORE— THIS PRETENDING, THIS LYING TO BA. I WILL NOT EAT MEAT WHILE BA AND BAPU ARE ALIVE.

ABOUT THIS TIME, MOHAN'S ELDER BROTHER GOT INTO DEBT. TO REPAY IT, THE TWO CLIPPED A BIT OF GOLD FROM HIS ARMLET.

THAT EVENING, THEIR PARENTS NOTICED IT. THERE WERE QUESTIONS.

I DON'T KNOW EITHER.

I...I... THE PIECE FELL OFF... I DON'T KNOW WHERE...

THE THEFT AND THE LIE LAY LIKE A DOUBLE WEIGHT ON MOHAN.

I CANNOT CARRY THIS GUILT WITHIN ME ALL MY LIFE. I CANNOT.

HE WROTE DOWN HIS CONFESSION ON A PIECE OF PAPER AND GAVE IT TO HIS FATHER WHO LAY ILL.

SO BAPU, YOUR SON IS NOW, IN YOUR EYES, NO BETTER THAN A COMMON THIEF ....

KARAMCHAND TORE UP THE PAPER AND LAY DOWN AGAIN. HE ONLY WEPT SILENTLY.

OH, BAPU, YOUR SILENT TEARS WOUND ME MORE THAN A SLAP MIGHT HAVE... THANK YOU, BAPU THANK YOU.

MOHAN SAW THAT LOVE COULD PUNISH MORE EFFECTIVELY THAN VIOLENCE, AND THAT IT PURIFIED THE PERSON PUNISHED. IT WAS AN OBJECT LESSON IN AHIMSA.

THIS LESSON IN AHIMSA BECAME A MORAL IDEAL FOR MOHAN WHEN HE READ THE FOLLOWING VERSES BY THE GUJARATI POET, SHAMAL BHATT:

FOR A BOWL OF WATER, GIVE IN RETURN A GOODLY MEAL. A GOOD TURN DESERVES ONE TEN TIMES AS GOOD WITH ALL ONE'S HEART. THEY WHO RETURN GOOD FOR EVIL; THEY HAVE TRULY WON THE BATTLE FOR LIFE.

FOLLOWING THE IDEAL, MOHAN INDEED WON THE BATTLE OF LIFE AND BECAME ONE OF THE GREATEST OF MEN IN THE HISTORY OF THE WORLD.

OFTEN, MEMBERS OF MOHAN'S FAMILY AND VISITORS OF VARIOUS FAITHS WOULD GATHER ROUND TO DISCUSS THEIR DIFFERENT POINTS OF VIEW WITH KARAMCHAND. MOHAN LISTENED TO THEM KEENLY.

THESE DISCUSSIONS HELPED MOHAN TO DEVELOP EQUAL RESPECT FOR ALL RELIGIONS.

THE ONE PRINCIPLE COMMON TO ALL RELIGIONS WAS TRUTH WITH WHICH MOHAN HAD FALLEN IN LOVE AS A CHILD.

I MUST KNOW THE TRUTH, AND ALWAYS LIVE BY IT.

MOHAN'S FAITH IN TRUTH GREW STRONGER FROM YEAR TO YEAR. MANY YEARS LATER HE WAS TO SAY, "TRUTH IS GOD. IT IS A GOD ANYONE CAN WORSHIP, EVEN AN ATHEIST".

KARAMCHAND, AILING FOR A LONG TIME, DIED IN 1885. PLANS HAD TO BE MADE FOR HIS SONS. IT WAS DECIDED THAT MOHAN SHOULD GO TO ENGLAND AND PREPARE FOR A CAREER IN LAW.

BA, DON'T LOOK SO SAD. BEFORE BOTH BECHARJI MAHARAJ AND YOU, I TAKE THIS VOW: I WILL NOT TOUCH WINE, WOMEN OR MEAT.

DON'T GO...

I MUST, DEAR, FOR OUR FUTURE.

IN BOMBAY, MOHAN'S COMMUNITY THREATENED HIM WITH EXCOMMUNICATION IF HE 'CROSSED THE WATERS'. BUT HE HAD SET HIS HEART ON GOING, AND HE WENT.

IN ENGLAND, EVERYTHING APPEARED STRANGE AND FASCINATING TO MOHAN. IN THE HOTEL LIFT —

IS THIS A ROOM WHERE WE SIT FOR SOME TIME BEFORE WE ARE TAKEN TO OUR ROOMS?

HE JOINED THE INNER TEMPLE OF THE INNS OF COURT IN LONDON.

MOHAN DID NOT BREAK THE VOW HE HAD MADE BEFORE HIS MOTHER.

GANDHI, IN THIS COLD CLIMATE, EITHER YOU TAKE MEAT OR WINE, OR IT IS DEATH.

MY VOW IS SUCH THAT I WILL HAVE TO OPT FOR DEATH !

HE READ A BOOK WHICH MADE HIM A VEGETARIAN BY CHOICE, WHEREAS BEFORE HE HAD BEEN ONE BY BIRTH AND FOR HIS PARENT'S SAKE. HE JOINED THE LONDON VEGETARIAN SOCIETY AND BEGAN TO RELISH BLAND VEGETARIAN FOOD.

HOW GOOD THIS PLAIN BOILED SPINACH TASTES. IT IS TRUE; THE SEAT OF TASTE LIES NOT IN THE TONGUE, BUT IN THE MIND.

THUS BEGAN GANDHI'S LIFE-LONG INTEREST IN DISCOVERING THE RELATION OF FOOD WITH THE HEALTH OF BODY, MIND AND SOUL.

A PLEA FOR VEGETARIANISM BY HENRY SALT

FORGETTING HIS SCHOOL-DAY DISLIKE OF THE ENGLISH IN INDIA, GANDHI ADMIRED THE ENGLISH IN ENGLAND AND TRIED TO MAKE HIMSELF AN ENGLISH GENTLEMAN.

I'VE BEEN TRYING FOR TWENTY MINUTES. THIS TIE JUST WON'T GET ITSELF TIED!

HE TOOK DANCING AND VIOLIN LESSONS, AND JOINED ELOCUTION CLASSES.

THEN ONE DAY, HE SUDDENLY AWOKE FROM THE FALSE DREAM AND DECIDED TO REMAIN INDIAN AND CONCENTRATE ON HIS STUDIES.

A LITTLE LATER, TWO ENGLISH THEOSOPHIST FRIENDS INTRODUCED GANDHI TO TWO OF SIR EDWIN ARNOLD'S BOOKS....

THE SONG CELESTIAL

A translation of the Bhagavad Geeta in English verse

ASIA

...AND A CHRISTIAN ACQUAINTANCE GAVE HIM THE BIBLE TO READ. "THE SERMON ON THE MOUNT" APPEALED TO GANDHI GREATLY.

ALL THREE BOOKS TEACH THE SAME TRUTH THAT RENUNCIATION IS THE HIGHEST FORM OF RELIGION.

GANDHI, EVEN WHILE BEING INDIAN, NOW BECAME A CITIZEN OF BOTH, THE EAST AND THE WEST.

THEN IN 1891, HE RETURNED TO INDIA, A FULL-FLEDGED BARRISTER. AFTER HE LANDED IN BOMBAY—

MANU, BA IS DEAD. BUT SHE DIED KNOWING THAT YOU HAVE PASSED.

BA... MY BELOVED BA.

GANDHI CONTROLLED HIS GRIEF. LIFE HAD TO GO ON.

HE SET UP PRACTICE. BUT HIS SHYNESS HAD NOT LEFT HIM, AND IN A LAW COURT IN BOMBAY, ONE DAY—

SPEAK UP! ... WHY MR. GANDHI, YOU CANNOT UTTER A WORD! WHAT KIND OF A BARRISTER WILL YOU MAKE?

FOR ALMOST TWO YEARS, GANDHI GOT NO WORK. THEN IN 1893, THERE CAME AN OFFER FROM SOME MERCHANTS OF PORBANDAR TO GO TO SOUTH AFRICA AS THEIR LAWYER. GANDHI SEIZED THE OPPORTUNITY AND SET SAIL. SOON—

DURBAN, NATAL. HOW BEAUTIFUL IT LOOKS, LIT UP BY THE SUN.

GANDHI SET FOOT IN THIS COUNTRY OF COALMINES AND SUGAR PLANTATIONS; OF BOUNTIFUL FRUIT AND GRAIN. HIS EMPLOYER, DADA ABDULLA SHETH, WAS THERE TO RECEIVE HIM.

ONE LOOK TOLD GANDHI THE WHOLE STORY. IN THIS RICH LAND, THERE WAS POVERTY— THE POVERTY OF HUMANENESS.

IN THE SECOND WEEK AFTER HIS ARRIVAL, HE TRAVELLED ON WORK TO PRETORIA, CAPITAL CITY OF THE TRANSVAAL. AND HE CAME FACE TO FACE WITH THE INHUMANITY OF SOUTH AFRICA.

HEY, COOLIE! YOU CAN'T SIT HERE. GO TO THE VAN COMPARTMENT.

BUT I HOLD A FIRST CLASS TICKET. THIS IS MY RIGHTFUL SEAT. I WILL NOT GO.

YOU WON'T, EH? WE'LL SEE ABOUT THAT.

GANDHI SAT IN THE DARK WAITING ROOM, NOT ONLY SHIVERING WITH COLD, BUT ALSO TREMBLING WITH HUMILIATION.

SHALL I TAKE THE NEXT SHIP BACK TO INDIA? NO... I WILL STAY, SUFFER THE INSULTS, AND FIGHT THE COLOUR PREJUDICE AGAINST INDIANS.

PIETERMARITZBURG

THE EXPERIENCES CAME THICK AND FAST. IN THE TRANSVAAL, COLOUR PREJUDICE WAS EVEN STRONGER THAN IN NATAL.

SO YOU REFUSE TO SIT AT MY FEET, EH, SAMI*... YOU COOLIE!

AT NIGHT, GANDHI ARRIVED AT JOHANNESBURG. HE WENT TO A HOTEL.

SORRY, NO ROOM.

GRAND NATIONAL HOTEL

IN PRETORIA, HE WAS KICKED FOR WALKING ON THE FOOTPATH IN FRONT OF PRESIDENT KRUGER'S HOUSE.

GANDHI GOT TOGETHER A GROUP OF INDIAN MERCHANTS IN PRETORIA. THEY MET OFTEN TO DISCUSS THEIR PROBLEMS. BUT GANDHI CONCENTRATED FIRST ON FINISHING THE LEGAL WORK HE HAD COME TO DO. HE SOON COMPLETED IT.

I'M GLAD YOU HAVE DECIDED THE CASE OUT OF COURT, ABDULLABHAI. IT'S OVER AND DONE WITH NOW, AND I CAN GO HOME.

TO SHOW MY GRATITUDE, I WOULD LIKE TO ARRANGE A FARE-WELL PARTY FOR YOU.

AND DURING THE PARTY, GANDHI SAW IT!

WHAT! THEY ARE PASSING A LAW THAT WILL TAKE AWAY THE VOTING RIGHTS OF INDIANS?

NATAL MERCURY

Indian Franchise

* CONTEMPTUOUS TERM FOR INDIANS — A CORRUPTION OF "SWAMI"

IT WAS AS IF ALL THE INSULTS HE AND THE INDIAN COMMUNITY SUFFERED STOOD TELESCOPED IN THAT SMALL CORNER OF THE NEWSPAPER.

TAKING AWAY OUR VOTING RIGHTS STRIKES AT THE ROOT OF OUR SELF-RESPECT. YOU MUST FIGHT IT.

GANDHIBHAI, WE ARE UNEDUCATED MEN. WHAT DO WE UNDERSTAND OF THESE MATTERS? BUT IF YOU COULD STAY BACK AND GUIDE US, WE WILL FIGHT.

ALL RIGHT, I WILL DELAY MY DEPARTURE.

AH!... ALLAH IS GREAT AND MERCIFUL.

AND THE PARTY TRANSFORMED ITSELF INTO A PUBLIC COMMITTEE. A POLITE, BUT FIRM PETITION WAS DRAWN UP AND SENT TO THE LEGISLATIVE ASSEMBLY.

AND ON THE THIRD DAY OF THE READING OF THE BILL, FOR THE FIRST TIME, THE LEGISLATIVE ASSEMBLY HALL SAW A STRANGE RUSH—OF INDIANS—SUDDENLY CONSCIOUS OF THEIR RIGHTS.

MOST OF THE NEWSPAPERS JUSTIFIED THE BILL. THE 'NATAL MERCURY' WROTE —

THE ASIATIC IS A POLITICAL INFANT OF THE MOST BACKWARD TYPE. INDIANS ARE PARASITICAL. IT IS AN INJUSTICE TO GIVE THEM FRANCHISE AT ALL...

GANDHI REPLIED —

INDIANS COME OF ONE OF THE MOST CIVILISED RACES IN THE WORLD. THEY HAVE EXERCISED THE VOTE LONG BEFORE THE ENGLISH KNEW OF VOTING. NOTHING IS SO WELL ORGANISED AND SO ESSENTIALLY REPRESENTATIVE AS INDIAN VILLAGE COMMUNITY. AND THE INDIANS COMING HERE AS LABOURERS, FAR FROM BEING PARASITICAL, HAVE HELPED TO BUILD NATAL TO PROSPERITY.

THE GOVERNMENT WAS ALARMED. A PROUD INDIAN VOICE HAD RAISED ITSELF. YET THE VOICE SPOKE SO JUSTLY AND WITHOUT AGGRESSIVENESS, THAT SOME PAPERS EVEN PRAISED IT.

NATAL MERCURY WROTE: WE MUST ADMIT THAT THE INDIANS MAKE OUT A VERY GOOD CASE FROM THEIR POINT OF VIEW.

IN SPITE OF THIS, THE INDIANS, LED BY GANDHI, HAD TO CARRY ON A LONG-DRAWN-OUT STRUGGLE FOR THEIR RIGHTS. IN AUGUST 1894, THE NATAL INDIAN CONGRESS WAS BORN. ENCOURAGED FROM LONDON BY DADABHAI NAOROJI, GANDHI BEGAN HIS 20-YEAR WAR ON SOUTH AFRICAN RACISM.

AND WHEN GANDHI WENT TO INDIA TO BRING BACK HIS FAMILY, HE SPOKE AT MEETINGS TO INTEREST INDIANS IN THE CAUSE OF SOUTH AFRICAN INDIANS.

THEY TREAT US WITH CONTEMPT. SUBMISSION TO THESE INSULTS MEANS DEGRADATION.

GANDHI HAD NOT SAID ANYTHING IN INDIA THAT HE HAD NOT ALREADY SPOKEN OUT LOUD AND CLEAR IN SOUTH AFRICA. YET WHEN HE RETURNED TO DURBAN IN 1897 —

HOW DARE YOU CONDEMN US IN INDIA! TAKE THAT...

...AND THAT!

STOP IT! LEAVE THE POOR MAN ALONE!

THE POLICE SUPERINTENDENT'S WIFE, MRS. ALEXANDER, SHIELDED HIM FROM THE BLOWS.

THE POLICE ARRIVED AND MANAGED TO TAKE HIM TO HIS FRIEND PARSEE RUSTOMJI'S HOUSE, BUT THE CROWD FOLLOWED. SUPERINTENDENT ALEXANDER TRIED TO HUMOUR THE CROWD.

WE'LL HANG OLD GANDHI FROM THE SOUR APPLE TREE...

MEANWHILE, POLICE DETECTIVES, DRESSED AS INDIANS, SECRETLY ESCORTED GANDHI TO THE POLICE STATION.

MR. ESCOMBE, NATAL'S ATTORNEY-GENERAL, CAME TO SEE GANDHI.

YOU ARE BADLY WOUNDED. NAME YOUR ASSAILANTS. I WILL HAVE THEM ARRESTED AND PROSECUTED.

NO, I DON'T WANT TO PROSECUTE ANYONE. THEY ARE NOT TO BLAME. THEIR LEADERS AND A RACIST SOCIETY ARE TO BLAME.

GANDHI CONTINUED HIS NON-AGGRESSIVE POLICY. HE EVEN FORMED AN INDIAN AMBULANCE CORPS DURING THE WAR IN 1899 BETWEEN ENGLAND AND THE BOER* COLONIES OF THE TRANSVAAL TO THE NORTH AND THE ORANGE FREE STATE TO THE WEST OF NATAL.

BY CARRYING THEIR WOUNDED FROM THE FIELD, WE WILL DEMONSTRATE TO THE ENGLISH THAT WE ARE ONE WITH THEM AND SO, ONE OF THEM...

...FOR GANDHI BELIEVED AT THIS TIME THAT THE BRITISH EMPIRE, WITH ALL ITS DEFECTS AND FAULTS, WAS ON THE WHOLE FOR THE GOOD OF MANKIND.

AFTER THE WAR, GANDHI RETURNED TO INDIA IN DECEMBER 1901, AND ATTENDED THE CONGRESS SESSION IN CALCUTTA. HE STAYED WITH GOPAL KRISHNA GOKHALE AND BECAME A CLOSE FRIEND AND FOLLOWER OF HIS.

CONGRESS SESSION CALCUTTA

BEFORE THE YEAR 1902 WAS OUT, GANDHI WAS RECALLED TO SOUTH AFRICA BY HIS INDIAN FRIENDS THERE.

THOUGH THE BOERS WERE DEFEATED BY THE BRITISH, THE PREJUDICE AGAINST INDIANS REMAINED AS STRONG AS BEFORE AND THE BRITISH OFFICIALS, WHO RULED THE CONQUERED COLONIES, ENFORCED OLD LAWS AGAINST THE INDIANS MORE STRICTLY THAN THE FORMER BOER GOVERNMENT.

ON HIS RETURN, GANDHI SETTLED IN THE TRANSVAAL'S PREMIER CITY, JOHANNESBURG. IN HIS HOUSE HERE, LATER, HIS ENGLISH FRIEND HENRY POLAK, HIS SERVANT, AND INDIAN VISITORS, OFTEN LIVED TOGETHER WITH GANDHI'S OWN FAMILY AS MEMBERS OF A LARGE FAMILY.

* THE BOERS WERE THE DESCENDANTS OF DUTCH SETTLERS.

ONE DAY, POLAK GAVE GANDHI A BOOK, "UNTO THIS LAST" BY THE GREAT WRITER, JOHN RUSKIN.

RUSKIN TEACHES THAT THE GOOD OF THE INDIVIDUAL LIES IN THE GOOD OF ALL; THAT A LIFE OF LABOUR AND SIMPLICITY, CLOSE TO NATURE, IS THE LIFE WORTH LIVING.

THE BOOK CAST A MAGIC SPELL ON GANDHI. THE NEXT DAY, HE DECIDED TO PUT RUSKIN'S IDEALS...

...INTO PRACTICE. A FEW KILOMETRES AWAY FROM DURBAN IN NATAL, GANDHI CHOSE A SITE FOR HIS FIRST ASHRAM NAMED PHOENIX AFTER A RAILWAY STATION OF THAT NAME NEAR BY.

IN JUNE 1903, WITH THE HELP OF A FRIEND, GANDHI HAD STARTED A WEEKLY, "INDIAN OPINION" TO CARRY ON HIS FIGHT AGAINST RACIAL LAWS. THE WEEKLY AND THE PRESS WERE REMOVED FROM DURBAN TO THE PHOENIX ASHRAM.

GANDHI'S FAMILY, HIS NEPHEWS, MAGANLAL AND CHHAGANLAL GANDHI, WITH THEIR FAMILIES, THREE ENGLISH FRIENDS AND AN INDIAN WORKER IN THE PRESS, JOINED THE ASHRAM.

THEY BUILT SIMPLE HOUSES FOR THEMSELVES, TILLED THE LAND, AND WORKED FOR "INDIAN OPINION" FOR VERY SMALL PAYMENT.

IN SPITE OF THE INJUSTICES SUFFERED BY THE INDIANS, GANDHI ONCE AGAIN HELPED THE GOVERNMENT IN ITS HOUR OF NEED. WHEN IN 1906, SOME NATIVE AFRICANS CALLED ZULUS WERE PROVOKED INTO REBELLION BY AN UNJUST TAX IMPOSED ON THEM BY THE NATAL GOVERNMENT, GANDHI ORGANISED A STRETCHER BEARER CORPS OF TWENTY-FOUR INDIANS TO REMOVE THE WOUNDED FROM THE BATTLEFIELD. THEIR MAIN DUTY WAS TO NURSE THE WOUNDED ZULUS...

...WHOM THE EUROPEAN VOLUNTEERS AND NURSES REFUSED TO LOOK AFTER. THIS SERVICE PLEASED GANDHI VERY MUCH AND THE INDIANS DID THEIR WORK WITH GREAT CARE AND SYMPATHY.

THIS EXPERIENCE OF HUMANITARIAN SERVICE WAS A TURNING POINT IN GANDHI'S PERSONAL LIFE. AROUND THIS TIME HE REALISED THE NEED FOR SELF-DISCIPLINE.

I WILL HAVE MORE AND MORE OPPORTUNITIES OF RENDERING SUCH SERVICE. I CANNOT DO FULL JUSTICE TO THEM IF AT THE SAME TIME I GO AFTER PLEASURES, HAVE MORE CHILDREN AND THE PROBLEMS OF FAMILY LIFE TO LOOK AFTER.

AND SO, AFTER DISCUSSING THE IDEA WITH KASTURBA, GANDHI TOOK THE VOW OF COMPLETE CELIBACY FOR THE REST OF HIS LIFE. THIS SENSE OF SELF-DISCIPLINE AND SACRIFICE WOULD STAND HIM IN GOOD STEAD FOR THE TASK AHEAD OF HIM.

AS SOON AS THE ZULU REBELLION WAS OVER, THE TRANSVAAL GOVERNMENT REWARDED THE INDIAN COMMUNITY FOR ITS SERVICE WITH A PROPOSAL - WITH A VERY HUMILIATING LAW. IT REQUIRED EVERY INDIAN TO TAKE OUT A REGISTRATION CERTIFICATE, GIVING, LIKE A CRIMINAL, HIS THUMB AND FINGER IMPRESSIONS ON THE APPLICATION. GANDHI CALLED A MEETING OF INDIANS IN JOHANNESBURG'S EMPIRE THEATRE.

LET US TAKE THIS PLEDGE; WE SOLEMNLY DECLARE, WITH GOD AS WITNESS, THAT WE WILL NEVER SUBMIT TO THIS HUMILIATING LAW.

GANDHI WAS THRILLED WITH PRIDE. HE ROSE AND SPOKE.

TO PLEDGE OURSELVES... IN THE NAME OF GOD OR WITH HIM AS WITNESS IS NOT SOMETHING TO BE TRIFLED WITH... EVERYONE MUST BE TRUE TO HIS PLEDGE, EVEN UNTO DEATH, NO MATTER WHAT OTHERS DO. EVEN IF ALL OTHERS GO BACK ON THE PLEDGE AND I AM LEFT ALONE, I WILL DIE, BUT NEVER SUBMIT TO THE LAW.

A THRILL WENT THROUGH EVERY MAN IN THE HALL. THIS WAS THE VOICE OF A GENERAL CALLING HIS TROOPS TO A NEW KIND OF WAR. THEY ROSE TO A MAN.

WITH GOD AS WITNESS, WE PLEDGE THAT WE WILL NEVER SUBMIT TO THIS LAW, AND WILL SUFFER THE PENALTY FOR DISOBEYING IT.

A NEW FORCE IN HUMAN HISTORY WAS BORN ON THIS 11TH DAY OF SEPTEMBER 1906. IN LESS THAN FIFTY YEARS, IT WAS TO FREE INDIA FROM THE IMPERIAL RULE OF BRITAIN, AND THEN, ONE AFTER ANOTHER, THE OTHER COUNTRIES OF ASIA AND AFRICA HELD IN BONDAGE BY EUROPEAN COLONIAL POWERS.

THIS STRUGGLE WAS CALLED 'PASSIVE RESISTANCE'. BUT GANDHI DID NOT LIKE THE PHRASE. IT DID NOT EXPRESS THE ACTIVE MORAL POWER OF THE NEW WEAPON. HE ADVERTISED A PRIZE FOR ANOTHER SUITABLE NAME.

MY NEPHEW MAGANLAL HAS SUGGESTED IN HIS LETTER THE NAME OF 'SADAGRAHA'- FIRMNESS IN A GOOD CAUSE. AN EXCELLENT NAME; BUT I WILL MAKE A SMALL MODIFICATION.

WE ARE FIGHTING INJUSTICE AND OPPRESSION WITH THE SPIRITUAL WEAPON OF TRUTH. WE WILL THEREFORE CALL IT 'SATYAGRAHA'- FIRMNESS IN FIGHTING INJUSTICE BY SCRUPULOUSLY TRUTHFUL MEANS.

THE NEW LAW WAS PASSED IN MARCH 1907. THE SATYAGRAHA AGAINST IT COMMENCED IN JULY. THE MAJORITY OF INDIANS REFUSED TO APPLY FOR THE CERTIFICATES. LEADING INDIANS, INCLUDING GANDHI, WERE JAILED. BUT NO ONE WEAKENED IN HIS RESOLVE. INDIANS, PREVIOUSLY FRIGHTENED BY THE VERY WORD 'JAIL', HAD, INSPIRED BY GANDHI, LOST ALL FEAR OF IT. THEY CALLED THEIR PRISON "HIS MAJESTY'S HOTEL".

GANDHI WON THIS FIRST BATTLE OF HIS NONVIOLENT FIGHT. GENERAL SMUTS, THE HOME MINISTER, ACCEPTED THE OFFER GANDHI HAD MADE BEFORE STARTING THE SATYAGRAHA...

...THAT THE INDIANS WOULD VOLUNTARILY TAKE OUT THE NEW REGISTRATION CERTIFICATES, AND GIVE THEIR FINGER IMPRESSIONS IF THEY WERE NOT FORCED TO DO SO BY A LAW.

MANY INDIANS DID NOT LIKE THE COMPROMISE. THEY DID NOT UNDERSTAND THE DIFFERENCE BETWEEN VOLUNTARY AND COMPULSORY REGISTRATION. ONE OF THEM, A PATHAN CLIENT OF GANDHI, NAMED MIR ALAM, ASSAULTED GANDHI AS GANDHI WAS GOING TO THE PERMIT OFFICE TO APPLY FOR THE CERTIFICATE.

HEY, RAMA.

BUT THIS TIME ALSO, GANDHI FOLLOWED THE LAW OF AHIMSA. HE WROTE TO THE ATTORNEY GENERAL SAYING THAT HIS ASSAILANTS SHOULD NOT BE PROSECUTED.

THE WOUNDED GANDHI WAS TAKEN BY A NOBLE MISSIONARY, JOSEPH DOKE*, TO HIS HOUSE AND NURSED WITH LOVING CARE. AT GANDHI'S REQUEST HIS LITTLE DAUGHTER, OLIVE, SANG GANDHI'S FAVOURITE ENGLISH HYMN BY CARDINAL NEWMAN.

LEAD, KINDLY LIGHT, AMID THE ENCIRCLING GLOOM, LEAD THOU ME ON...

LIKE SOME INDIANS, MANY EUROPEANS ALSO DID NOT LIKE THE COMPROMISE. UNDER PRESSURE FROM THEM, SMUTS DID NOT REPEAL THE REGISTRATION ACT IN THE MANNER GANDHI AND HIS INDIAN SUPPORTERS WANTED. IN PROTEST, THE INDIANS WHO HAD TAKEN OUT THE VOLUNTARY CERTIFICATES MADE A BONFIRE OF THEM.

* THE NEXT YEAR, IN 1909, HE WROTE GANDHI'S FIRST BIOGRAPHY— "M.K. GANDHI, AN INDIAN PATRIOT IN SOUTH AFRICA".— REPRINTED IN INDIA BY THE PUBLICATIONS DIVISION, GOVERNMENT OF INDIA.

THE SECOND SATYAGRAHA WENT ON FOR THREE YEARS. THE SATYAGRAHI PRISONERS WERE TREATED VERY HARSHLY; MADE TO BREAK STONES, DIG FIELDS AND CLEAN LATRINES.

BUT SATYAGRAHIS' SPIRIT REMAINED UNBROKEN.

EVEN GANDHI WAS NOT SPARED; HE WAS KEPT FOR SOME TIME IN A DARK, NARROW, SOLITARY CELL, AND ASKED TO DO HARD LABOUR.

GANDHI BORE IT ALL WITHOUT ILL-WILL OR ANGER. LATER IN INDIA, HIS PRISONER'S CAP, WITH CHANGES, WOULD BECOME THE NATIONAL KHADI "GANDHI CAP".

WHILE GANDHI WAS IN PRISON, KASTURBA FELL ILL. HE WROTE TO HER FROM JAIL —

I AM VERY MUCH GRIEVED, BUT I AM NOT IN A POSITION TO GO THERE TO NURSE YOU... I CAN COME ONLY IF I PAY THE FINE WHICH I MUST NOT DO... I LOVE YOU SO DEARLY THAT EVEN IF YOU ARE DEAD, YOU WILL BE ALIVE TO ME... IF YOU DIE, YOUR DEATH ALSO WILL BE A SACRIFICE TO THE CAUSE OF SATYAGRAHA.

GANDHI WAS LATER RELEASED, THOUGH THE SATYAGRAHA CONTINUED. GANDHI STARTED ANOTHER ASHRAM IN THE TRANSVAAL CALLED TOLSTOY FARM, ON A LARGE PIECE OF LAND BOUGHT BY A GERMAN FRIEND, HERMAN KALLENBACH. ON THIS FARM, GANDHI WITH HIS WHOLE FAMILY AND THE FAMILIES OF SATYAGRAHIS IN JAIL LIVED A VERY SIMPLE LIFE OF FEW NEEDS AND LABOUR FOR ALL, ACCORDING TO THE IDEALS OF THE GREAT RUSSIAN WRITER, LEO TOLSTOY.

LATER IN LIFE, GANDHI REMEMBERED THE TWO AND A HALF YEARS ON TOLSTOY FARM, WITH ITS DISCIPLINE OF DAILY LABOUR, AS THE HAPPIEST PERIOD IN HIS LIFE. OUT OF THIS EXPERIENCE, GREW GANDHI'S FAMOUS SATYAGRAHA ASHRAM IN AHMEDABAD.

THE SECOND SATYAGRAHA HAD BEEN SUSPENDED IN MAY 1911, WHEN GENERAL SMUTS ASSURED GANDHI THAT THE GOVERNMENT WOULD MEET THE DEMANDS OF THE INDIANS. BUT GENERAL SMUTS DID NOT KEEP THE ASSURANCE HE HAD GIVEN TO GANDHI, AND THE THIRD AND LAST SATYAGRAHA IN SOUTH AFRICA STARTED IN SEPTEMBER 1913. THIS TIME, WOMEN SINGING DEVOTIONAL SONGS ALSO JOINED THE SATYAGRAHA...

LET NOT THY MIND BE AFFECTED BY JOY OR SORROW...

... WITH KASTURBA HERSELF GOING TO JAIL.

DURING THIS SATYAGRAHA, GANDHI HAD INCLUDED A NEW DEMAND THAT THE HEAVY, UNJUST TAX OF THREE POUNDS PER YEAR, WHICH INDENTURED LABOURERS SETTLED IN NATAL HAD TO PAY, SHOULD BE REMOVED. SO THE LABOURERS IN THE COAL-MINES ALSO JOINED THE STRUGGLE. THEY STRUCK WORK AND LEFT THE MINES WITH THEIR FAMILIES AND BELONGINGS. GANDHI LED THEM ALL, MORE THAN TWO THOUSAND IN NUMBER, IN A PEACEFUL MARCH FROM NATAL TO TRANSVAAL, WHICH INDIANS OUTSIDE COULD NOT ENTER.

GANDHI WAS ARRESTED.

AFTER GANDHI'S ARREST, THE GOVERNMENT TRIED TO BREAK THE STRIKE. THE LABOURERS WERE FLOGGED, SHOT AT, AND ASSAULTED BY MOUNTED POLICE.

THERE WAS AN OUTCRY IN INDIA. GOPAL KRISHNA GOKHALE AROUSED STRONG PUBLIC OPINION IN SUPPORT OF THE SATYA-GRAHIS AND EVEN THE VICEROY, LORD HARDINGE, PUBLICLY CONDEMNED THE REPRESSION.

WHEN GANDHI, AFTER HIS RELEASE, HEARD OF THE SUFFERINGS OF THE LABOURERS, HE DISCARDED HIS USUAL DRESS AND FOR SOME TIME ADOPTED A MOURNING DRESS OF A LOINCLOTH AND KURTA, AND SHAVED HIS HEAD.

AT LAST, THE GOVERNMENT YIELDED TO THE MORAL POWER OF SATYAGRAHA AND A FRIENDLY SMUTS CONCEDED ALL THE DEMANDS OF GANDHI IN A GENEROUS SPIRIT.

GREAT WAS THE REJOICING AMONG THE INDIANS. HIS WORK COMPLETE, GANDHI SAILED FOR INDIA VIA ENGLAND. BUT HE LEFT BEHIND A GIFT FOR GENERAL SMUTS - A PAIR OF SANDALS HE HAD MADE HIMSELF. YEARS LATER, SMUTS WAS TO SAY—

I AM NOT WORTHY TO STAND IN THE SHOES OF SO GREAT A MAN.

BUT WHILE IN SOUTH AFRICA, ONE POINT MADE BY A NEWSPAPER WRITER HAD BURST ON GANDHI LIKE A SHOCK WAVE. TRUE, SOUTH AFRICA CAST CONTEMPT ON THE PEOPLE FROM INDIA ...

...INDIA... THE CRADLE OF CIVILIZATION... BUT THE BULK OF THE INDIAN LABOURING CLASS IN SOUTH AFRICA... BEING MOSTLY LOWCASTE, ARE CONDEMNED TO BE A SERVILE RACE BY THE CASTE SYSTEM OF THE HINDOOS. SO THE EVIL FROM WHICH THEY SUFFER IS NOT FROM WITHOUT, BUT FROM WITHIN. IF THEN MR. GANDHI'S FELLOW COUNTRYMEN HAVE CONDEMNED THEMSELVES... TO A MENIAL LOT, HOW CAN HE EXPECT US TO HELP THEM?... HE HAD BETTER BEGIN HIS WORK AT HOME.

OH, GOD! THIS MAN'S ARROW HAS STRUCK MY HEART. YES, WE INDIANS HAVE OURSELVES BUILT OUR OWN PRISON WALLS.

BUT GANDHI WAS GOING HOME NOW. THERE HE MUST BEGIN HIS WORK.

ON JANUARY 9, 1915, A NEW GANDHI DISEMBARKED AT BOMBAY'S APOLLO BUNDAR. INWARDLY, HE ALREADY DEEPLY FELT HIMSELF AN INDIAN; EVEN OUTWARDLY NOW, HE BECAME INDIAN.

GOPAL KRISHNA GOKHALE, GANDHI'S "POLITICAL GUIDE" WAS IN BOMBAY ON THAT DAY. GANDHI CALLED ON HIM.

INDIA IS UNKNOWN TO YOU AND YOU TO HER. TRAVEL ACROSS HER LENGTH AND BREADTH TO GET TO KNOW HER. EXPRESS NO OPINION ON POLITICAL MATTERS FOR A YEAR.

SO FOR THE FIRST YEAR, GANDHI, WITH KASTURBA, TRAVELLED WIDELY THROUGH THE COUNTRY. HE SAW AND LIKED THE PEOPLE'S SIMPLICITY OF NATURE AND LIVING HABITS.

BUT HE ALSO SAW THEIR IGNORANCE AND THEIR INDIFFERENCE TO CLEANLINESS.

HE SAW THE FEAR AND HATRED OF THE RULERS AMONG EDUCATED YOUTH.

ABOVE ALL, HE SAW THE POVERTY OF THE MASSES.

WHILE TOURING, GANDHI SET UP IN MAY 1915, AN ASHRAM AT KOCHARAB, A VILLAGE ON THE OUTSKIRTS OF AHMEDABAD ON THE WESTERN BANK OF THE RIVER SABARMATI. HE NAMED IT "SATYAGRAHA ASHRAM". THE SENIOR MEMBERS OF THE ASHRAM DEDICATED THEMSELVES TO THE SERVICE OF THE COUNTRY AND TOOK EIGHT VOWS TO MAKE THEMSELVES FIT FOR IT.

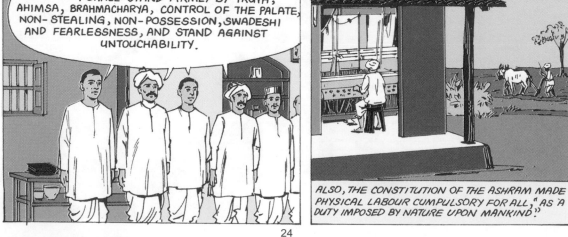

I SHALL STAND FIRMLY BY TRUTH, AHIMSA, BRAHMACHARYA, CONTROL OF THE PALATE, NON-STEALING, NON-POSSESSION, SWADESHI AND FEARLESSNESS, AND STAND AGAINST UNTOUCHABILITY.

ALSO, THE CONSTITUTION OF THE ASHRAM MADE PHYSICAL LABOUR CUMPULSORY FOR ALL, "AS A DUTY IMPOSED BY NATURE UPON MANKIND."

AS SOON AS HIS YEAR OF POLITICAL SILENCE WAS OVER, GANDHI WENT TO WORK. THE OCCASION: THE CELEBRATIONS IN FEBRUARY 1916, OF THE BANARAS HINDU UNIVERSITY FOUNDED BY PANDIT MADAN MOHAN MALAVIYA WITH THE HELP OF THE BRITISH THEOSOPHIST, MRS. ANNIE BESANT, WHO HAD ADOPTED INDIA AS HER MOTHERLAND.

BANARAS HINDU UNIVERSITY 1916

INVITED TO ADDRESS THE STUDENTS, GANDHI POURED OUT HIS HEART IN A PASSIONATE SPEECH ON WHAT HE HAD SEEN DURING HIS ONE YEAR'S TRAVELS.

I VISITED THE VISHWANATH TEMPLE IN KASHI* LAST EVENING... IS IT RIGHT THAT THE LANES OF OUR SACRED TEMPLE SHOULD BE AS DIRTY AS THEY ARE?... PEOPLE WALK ABOUT THE STREETS OF BOMBAY UNDER THE PERPETUAL FEAR OF DWELLERS IN THE MULTI-STOREYED BUILDINGS SPITTING UPON THEM...

AND HE SPOKE OF THE EXTREMES OF LUXURY AND POVERTY IN THE COUNTRY.

IN THE GREAT PANDAL♀ IN WHICH THE FOUNDATION CEREMONY WAS PERFORMED# BY THE VICEROY, WE WITNESSED AN EXHIBITION OF JEWELLERY WHICH MADE A SPLENDID FEAST FOR THE EYES... I COMPARE WITH THE RICHLY BEDECKED NOBLEMEN, THE MILLIONS OF THE POOR... WHENEVER I HEAR OF A GREAT PALACE RISING IN ANY GREAT CITY OF INDIA, I BECOME JEALOUS AT ONCE AND I SAY: "OH, IT IS THE MONEY THAT HAS COME FROM THE AGRICULTURISTS."

* VARANASI   ♀ A LARGE PAVILLION SET FOR A PUBLIC FUNCTION.
# ON FEBRUARY 4TH.

AND FINALLY, HE SPOKE OF THE ANARCHIST MOVEMENT SPREADING AMONG THE EDUCATED YOUTH IN THE COUNTRY.

I WOULD SAY TO THEM THAT THEIR ANARCHISM HAS NO ROOM IN INDIA IF INDIA IS TO CONQUER THE CONQUEROR. IT IS A SIGN OF FEAR... I HONOUR THE ANARCHIST FOR HIS BRAVERY IN BEING WILLING TO DIE FOR HIS COUNTRY: BUT I ASK HIM: IS KILLING HONOURABLE?

MRS. BESANT AND THE MAHARAJAS ON THE DAIS DID NOT LIKE GANDHI TALKING SO BOLDLY ABOUT ANARCHISM TO STUDENTS. THEY STOOD UP AND LEFT THE MEETING.

GANDHI ENDED HIS SPEECH ABRUPTLY AND THE MEETING BROKE UP IN CONFUSSION.

INDIA HEARD THIS FEARLESS VOICE AND KNEW THAT SOMEONE DIFFERENT HAD ENTERED THE SCENE. THE POET RABINDRANATH TAGORE GAVE HIM HIS PROPER NAME — MAHATMA, THE GREAT SOUL. AND THE POOR LOOKED UP TO HIM.

MAHATMAJI, I AM FROM CHAMPARAN DISTRICT, BIHAR. OUR ENGLISH LANDLORDS FORCED US TO GROW INDIGO. NOW THAT SYNTHETIC INDIGO HAS BEEN DISCOVERED THEY FORCE US TO PAY THEM COMPENSATION FOR NOT GROWING IT ANY LONGER. HELP US.

GANDHI WENT TO CHAMPARAN. THE GOVERNMENT ORDERED HIM TO LEAVE, WHICH HE REFUSED TO DO. HE WOULD INSTEAD GO WILLINGLY TO JAIL. THE NEWS SPREAD.

A LAWYER MAHATMA HAS COME, WHO IS GOING TO JAIL FOR OUR SAKE.

HE WANTS NOTHING FROM US; ONLY JUSTICE FOR US FROM THE ENGLISH.

AND THE VILLAGERS GATHERED IN CROWDS ROUND THE COURTHOUSE, STIRRED BY AN ANCIENT INDIAN MEMORY, DEAD NOW FOR CENTURIES, THAT A LEADER MUST BE FATHER TO HIS PEOPLE. HERE HE WAS — BAPU.*

BAPU...

BAPU...

BAPU...

GANDHI SUCCEEDED IN CONFOUNDING BOTH THE MAGISTRATE AND THE PLEADER AND WAS QUICKLY RELEASED. THEN QUIETLY, POLITELY, PAINSTAKINGLY, HE WORKED TO MAKE THE LANDLORDS RETURN PART OF WHAT THEY HAD FORCIBLY TAKEN FROM THE PEASANTS. HE HAD SHOWN THE PEASANTS, COWERING TILL NOW UNDER BRITISH AUTHORITY, THAT THEY NEED FEAR IT NO LONGER. IT WAS HERE THAT HE MET RAJENDRA PRASAD AND J.B. KRIPALANI.

* FATHER

GANDHI ALSO BEGAN A PROGRAMME OF CLEANLINESS IN CHAMPARAN'S VILLAGES, SWEEPING, CLEARING, TEACHING THE VILLAGERS THAT THERE IS DIGNITY IN CLEANING UP OUR OWN DIRT.

CHAMPARAN TOO TAUGHT HIM SOMETHING—THAT THE ENGLISH, THOUGH BASICALLY JUST, MUST LEAVE INDIA. FOR IN ORDER TO RULE HER, THEY BROKE HER BACK.

WHILE WORKING IN CHAMPARAN, GANDHI SHIFTED THE SATYAGRAHA ASHRAM FROM KOCHARAB TO ANOTHER SPOT TO THE NORTH, ALSO ON THE WESTERN BANK OF THE SABARMATI, CLOSE TO THE SABARMATI JAIL.

AN IDEAL SITE FOR THE JAIL-LOVING SATYAGRAHI. THE SABARMATI RIVER CONTINUES TO ADD BEAUTY TO IT.

GANDHI HAD BEAUTIFIED HIS ASHRAM EVEN MORE—A FAMILY OF 'UNTOUCHABLES' OR 'HARIJANS' * AS HE ADDRESSED THEM LATER, HAD JOINED THE ASHRAM AT KOCHARAB AND NOW LIVED WITH HIM.

LIFE IN THE ASHRAM FOLLOWED A STRICT DISCIPLINE OF FIXED HOURS OF PRAYER, MORNING AND EVENING. ONE OF THE SANSKRIT VERSES IN THE MORNING PRAYER WAS:

I DO NOT DESIRE EITHER KINGDOM OR HEAVEN OR FREEDOM FROM REBIRTH. I ONLY DESIRE END TO THE SUFFERINGS OF ALL CREATURES.

THE ASHRAM MEMBERS ALSO DID SEVERAL HOURS OF MANUAL LABOUR; BESIDES SPINNING AND WEAVING, SCAVENGING AND CLEANING LATRINES.

THIS WAS GANDHI'S WAY OF TRAINING HIS NON-VIOLENT ARMY OF VOLUNTEERS TO FEEL ONE WITH THE LOWEST CLASS IN SOCIETY.

* LITERALLY PEOPLE OF GOD, THE TERM FIRST USED BY RAMANUJACHARYA AND LATER NARSI MEHTA, BEFORE MAHATMA GANDHI.

GANDHI NEXT TOOK UP THE CAUSE OF AHMEDABAD'S POORLY PAID MILL WORKERS WHO WERE ASKING FOR A RAISE IN WAGES. THEY PLEDGED TO CONTINUE THE STRIKE TILL THE MILL-OWNERS AGREED TO THE RAISE.

THE OWNERS STOOD FIRM. THE WORKERS BEGAN TO TIRE. GANDHI WAS UPSET; THEY MUST NOT GIVE UP NOW. HOW COULD HE CONVINCE THEM?

IT IS TO THEIR GOOD TO STAY UNITED. MY BELOVED BA USED TO FAST FOR OUR GOOD...

AND THE NEXT MOMENT—

FRIENDS, UNDER OUR EK TEK* TREE, I ANNOUNCE THIS: I SHALL NOT TOUCH FOOD BECAUSE YOU ARE NOT UNITED IN YOUR PLEDGE.

BAPU, NO! DO NOT DO THIS; NOT FOR OUR SAKE.

FOR THE FIRST TIME, THROUGH A FAST, THROUGH SELF-DENIAL, A LEADER WAS PLAYING A DEEPLY PERSONAL ROLE, OF PARENT TO HIS CHILDREN.

THIS FAST IS NOT TO BLACKMAIL THE MILL-OWNERS. I HAVE CLEARLY TOLD THEM THAT. IT IS FOR THE WELFARE OF THE WORKERS.

FINALLY, THE MILL-OWNERS RELENTED. IT WAS AS IF THEY HAD BEEN REMINDED THAT IT WAS ONLY A PATERNAL EMPLOYER WHO REALLY SUCCEEDED.

AFTER THIS CAME THE ISSUE OF THE CULTIVATORS OF KHEDA DISTRICT TO THE SOUTH-EAST OF AHMEDABAD. OWING TO EXCESSIVE RAIN DURING THE PREVIOUS MONSOON, THE CROPS HAD FALLEN BELOW THE NORMAL LEVEL.

THE PEOPLE DEMANDED THAT THE COLLECTION OF LAND REVENUE SHOULD BE POSTPONED TO THE NEXT YEAR. BUT THE GOVERNMENT DID NOT AGREE TO THIS.

GANDHI ADVISED THE CULTIVATORS NOT TO PAY THE LAND REVENUE. THE GOVERNMENT CONFISCATED THE CATTLE THE HOUSEHOLD GOODS...

... AND EVEN THE STANDING CROPS IN THE FIELDS OF THOSE WHO DID NOT PAY.

* EK TEK – 'ONE PLEDGE'.

THIS RESULTED IN MUCH SUFFERING AMONG THE FARMERS, TILL, UNDER PRESSURE FROM THE VICEROY, THE GOVERNMENT OF BOMBAY CHANGED ITS POLICY AND THE COLLECTOR OF KHEDA INFORMED GANDHI THAT THE CULTIVATORS WHO WERE TOO POOR TO PAY WOULD NOT BE FORCED TO DO SO. THE FIGHT WAS THE BEGINNING OF THE EDUCATION OF THE PEOPLE OF GUJARAT IN SATYAGRAHA, A LESSON IN COURAGE AND SELF-SACRIFICE. AND IT GAVE THEM A NEW LEADER, VALLABHBHAI PATEL WHO BECAME GANDHI'S LOYAL LIEUTENANT IN ALL HIS SATYAGRAHA BATTLES.

SOON AFTER THIS, ALTHOUGH LOKAMANYA TILAK WAS AGAINST IT, GANDHI HELPED ENGLAND RECRUIT SOLDIERS FOR WORLD WAR-I. THE MESSAGE WAS CLEAR— DO UNTO US AS WE DO UNTO YOU. INDIA WANTED HOME RULE IN FAIR EXCHANGE FOR HER WAR EFFORTS. BUT, AT THE END OF THE WAR—

THE BRITISH HAVE PASSED THE ROWLATT ACTS TO KILL THE PEOPLE'S SPIRIT OF FREEDOM. THE HARSH WAR-TIME MEASURES ARE TO CONTINUE.

IS THIS OUR REWARD FOR ALL THE BLOOD INDIANS SPILT FOR THEM IN THE WAR?

IN PROTEST, GANDHI TOOK HIS FIRST MAJOR POLITICAL STEP IN INDIA. HE CALLED FOR A NATION-WIDE SATYAGRAHA; A HARTAL. ALL SHOPS, BUSINESS ESTABLISHMENTS, MILLS AND FACTORIES WERE TO BE VOLUNTARILY CLOSED ON SUNDAY, APRIL 6, 1919. THE CALL WAS FOLLOWED THROUGHOUT THE COUNTRY.

A NATION COMING PEACEFULLY TO A HALT WAS QUITE A SPECTACLE.

GANDHI WAS ARRESTED ON APRIL 9. AS A REACTION THERE WAS VIOLENCE IN SOME PLACES – DELHI, AMRITSAR, AHMEDABAD AND VIRAMGAM*. GANDHI WAS DEEPLY PAINED.

WHAT A GREAT BLOT ON SATYAGRAHA! I HAVE MADE A HIMALAYAN MIS-CALCULATION. I BELIEVED WRONGLY THAT THE PEOPLE WOULD KEEP PERFECT PEACE.

HE CALLED OFF THE SATYAGRAHA.

* A TOWN NEAR AHMEDABAD.

THEN CAME APRIL 13, BAISAKHI, AND THE MASSACRE AT JALLIANWALA BAGH IN AMRITSAR. AN ARMY OFFICER, GENERAL DYER, ANGERED BY THE KILLING OF SOME ENGLISHMEN IN THE CITY AND THE ASSAULT ON AN ENGLISHWOMAN ON THE 10TH BY AN EXCITED CROWD, WANTED TO PUNISH THE PEOPLE. UNDER HIS ORDERS SEPOYS FIRED ON AN UNARMED CROWD AND KILLED MORE THAN A THOUSAND*PEOPLE AND WOUNDED MORE THAN THREE THOUSAND.

THE SOLDIERS FIRED 1650 ROUNDS IN TEN MINUTES, AND STOPPED ONLY WHEN THEY HAD NO MORE AMMUNITION.

ON APRIL 15, MARTIAL LAW WAS IMPOSED IN MANY PARTS OF THE PUNJAB. COLLEGE STUDENTS IN LAHORE WERE FORCED TO WALK SEVERAL MILES IN THE HOT SUN TO ATTEND CUMPULSORY ROLL CALL TWICE A DAY.

SOME WERE FLOGGED IN PUBLIC.

AND THE PEOPLE PASSING THROUGH THE STREET IN WHICH THE ENGLISHWOMAN WAS ASSAULTED WERE FORCED TO CRAWL ON THEIR BELLIES.

ONE DISTRICT WAS BOMBED FROM THE AIR.

RESPECTABLE CITIZENS WERE ARRESTED WITHOUT WARRANT AND HANDCUFFED.

THE REIGN OF TERROR LASTED SIX WEEKS. BECAUSE OF THE MARTIAL LAW, FOR MANY DAYS, THE REST OF THE COUNTRY DID NOT KNOW WHAT WAS HAPPENING IN THE PUNJAB. BUT SLOWLY THE HORROR STORIES SPREAD, AND THE PEOPLE WERE SHOCKED.

* THE BRITISH GAVE THE FIGURES AS 379 KILLED AND OVER 1,200 WOUNDED.

GANDHI WAS NOT ALLOWED TO GO TO PUNJAB FOR SEVERAL MONTHS. WHEN AT LAST HE WENT THERE IN OCTOBER, FIRST TO LAHORE AND THEN TO AMRITSAR, LARGE CROWDS WELCOMED HIM.

WRITING IN HIS MAGAZINE, NAVAJIVAN, GANDHI SAID —

PEOPLE WHO HAD SUFFERED MUCH, WASHED AWAY THEIR GRIEF WITH THE WATERS OF LOVE.

BUT SOON, IN DECEMBER 1919, KING GEORGE V MADE AN APPEAL TO THE PEOPLE OF INDIA AND HIS OFFICIALS IN THE GOVERNMENT.

FORGET THE PAST, AND CO-OPERATE IN WORKING THE NEW REFORMS ACT IN THE PROPER SPIRIT

GANDHI TRUSTED THE BRITISH AND WELCOMED THE PROPOSAL.

ON DECEMBER 29, AT THE INDIAN NATIONAL CONGRESS SESSION AT AMRITSAR, PRESIDED OVER BY MOTILAL NEHRU, A NEW SLOGAN BEGAN TO DOMINATE THE POLITICAL HORIZON.

MAHATMA GANDHI KI JAI!

GANDHI WAS ESTABLISHED AND ACKNOWLEDGED AS A LEADER OF THE NATION.

'I do not claim that I have not committed any mistakes, but this I claim that at any given time, I did what I considered right at that time.'

MAHATMA GANDHI — The Father of The Nation

THE TERRIBLE MASSACRE AT JALLIANWALA BAGH ON APRIL 13, 1919, SENT SHOCK WAVES THROUGHOUT THE COUNTRY GANDHI WAS ALLOWED TO GO TO PUNJAB IN OCTOBER. HE MET MANY PEOPLE AND TALKED WITH THEM AND HEARD OF THE CRUELTIES THEY HAD SUFFERED. STILL HE CONTINUED TO TRUST THE BRITISH. BUT IT TOOK HIM ONLY A FEW MONTHS MORE TO REALISE THAT NEITHER THE BRITISH IN INDIA NOR THE WHITEHALL HAD REPENTED OF THE ATROCITIES PERPETRATED BY GENERAL DYER. THE BRITISH GOVERNMENT IN ENGLAND ALSO BROKE ITS PROMISE TO THE MUSLIMS OF INDIA NOT TO PUNISH TURKEY FOR HAVING FOUGHT ON THE SIDE OF GERMANY IN THE WORLD WAR.

LOSING HIS FAITH OF MANY YEARS IN THE BRITISH PEOPLE'S SENSE OF JUSTICE, GANDHI NOW TURNED A DETERMINED REBEL AGAINST BRITISH RULE IN INDIA. HE CALLED IT 'SATANIC' AND ASKED HINDUS AND MUSLIMS TO UNITE AGAINST IT AND NOT CO-OPERATE WITH IT IN ANY WAY.

I AM NOT ANTI-BRITISH, BUT I AM ANTI-UNTRUTH AND ANTI-INJUSTICE. SO LONG AS THE GOVERNMENT SPELLS INJUSTICE, IT MAY REGARD ME AS ITS ENEMY; IMPLACABLE ENEMY.

PROCLAIM TO THE GOVERNMENT: "YOU MAY HANG US ON THE GALLOWS, YOU MAY SEND US TO PRISON, BUT YOU WILL GET NO CO-OPERATION FROM US."

THE NON-CO-OPERATION PROGRAMME LAUNCHED BY GANDHI WAS BASED ON HIS BELIEF IN NON-VIOLENCE. IT MEANT REFUSAL TO CO-OPERATE WITH THE BRITISH GOVERNMENT IN ANY MANNER AND INVOLVED THE BOYCOTT OF BRITISH COURTS, SCHOOLS AND COLLEGES, THE SURRENDERING OF BRITISH HONOURS AND TITLES, AND THE BOYCOTT OF BRITISH GOODS.

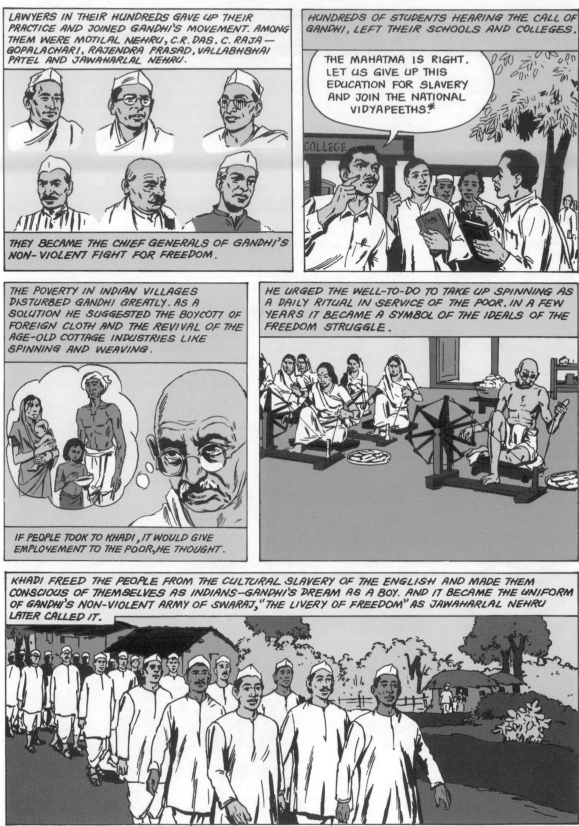

LAWYERS IN THEIR HUNDREDS GAVE UP THEIR PRACTICE AND JOINED GANDHI'S MOVEMENT. AMONG THEM WERE MOTILAL NEHRU, C.R. DAS, C. RAJA— GOPALACHARI, RAJENDRA PRASAD, VALLABHBHAI PATEL AND JAWAHARLAL NEHRU.

THEY BECAME THE CHIEF GENERALS OF GANDHI'S NON-VIOLENT FIGHT FOR FREEDOM.

HUNDREDS OF STUDENTS HEARING THE CALL OF GANDHI, LEFT THEIR SCHOOLS AND COLLEGES.

THE MAHATMA IS RIGHT. LET US GIVE UP THIS EDUCATION FOR SLAVERY AND JOIN THE NATIONAL VIDYAPEETHS.*

COLLEGE

THE POVERTY IN INDIAN VILLAGES DISTURBED GANDHI GREATLY. AS A SOLUTION HE SUGGESTED THE BOYCOTT OF FOREIGN CLOTH AND THE REVIVAL OF THE AGE-OLD COTTAGE INDUSTRIES LIKE SPINNING AND WEAVING.

IF PEOPLE TOOK TO KHADI, IT WOULD GIVE EMPLOYEMENT TO THE POOR, HE THOUGHT.

HE URGED THE WELL-TO-DO TO TAKE UP SPINNING AS A DAILY RITUAL IN SERVICE OF THE POOR. IN A FEW YEARS IT BECAME A SYMBOL OF THE IDEALS OF THE FREEDOM STRUGGLE.

KHADI FREED THE PEOPLE FROM THE CULTURAL SLAVERY OF THE ENGLISH AND MADE THEM CONSCIOUS OF THEMSELVES AS INDIANS—GANDHI'S DREAM AS A BOY. AND IT BECAME THE UNIFORM OF GANDHI'S NON-VIOLENT ARMY OF SWARAJ, "THE LIVERY OF FREEDOM" AS JAWAHARLAL NEHRU LATER CALLED IT.

* COLLEGES

GANDHI TRAVELLED OR A WHOLE YEAR THROUGHOUT THE COUNTRY TO PROPAGATE HIS IDEAS. AND THE MASSES WERE STIRRED BY HIS MESSAGE.

BOYCOTT FOREIGN CLOTH.

DOWN WITH BRITISH IMPERIALISM!

VANDE MATARAM.

INQUILAB ZINDABAD.

BUT PEOPLE HAD NOT YET LEARNT THE LESSON OF NON-VIOLENCE. ON THE ARRIVAL OF THE PRINCE OF WALES IN BOMBAY ON NOVEMBER 17, 1921, RIOTS BROKE OUT IN THE CITY.

THERE WERE VIOLENT INCIDENTS IN MADRAS IN JANUARY 1922, AND THEN IN CHAURI CHAURA NEAR GORAKHPUR IN UTTAR PRADESH IN FEBRUARY. AS IN APRIL 1919, THIS TIME ALSO GANDHI DECIDED TO SUSPEND THE NON-CO-OPERATION MOVEMENT.

THE SUDDEN SUSPENSION OF THE NON-CO-OPERATION MOVEMENT BY GANDHI, CAUSED CONFUSION AND DIVISION AMONG HIS FOLLOWERS. TAKING ADVANTAGE OF THE SITUATION, THE GOVERNMENT ARRESTED GANDHI ON MARCH 10. AT THE TRIAL —

I PLEAD GUILTY...I WANTED TO AVOID VIOLENCE...I KNOW THAT MY PEOPLE HAVE SOMETIMES GONE MAD. I AM DEEPLY SORRY FOR IT. I HAVE NO PERSONAL ILL-WILL AGAINST ANY SINGLE ADMINISTRATOR. BUT I HOLD IT TO BE A VIRTUE TO BE DISAFFECTED TOWARDS A GOVERNMENT WHICH HAS DONE MORE HARM TO INDIA THAN ANY PREVIOUS SYSTEM. I INVITE THE HIGHEST PENALTY.

MR. GANDHI, YOU ARE IN A DIFFERENT CATEGORY FROM ANY PERSON I HAVE EVER TRIED OR AM LIKELY TO TRY. I SENTENCE YOU TO SIX YEARS' IMPRISONMENT. IF THE GOVERNMENT LATER SEES FIT TO REDUCE THE TERM, NO ONE WOULD BE BETTER PLEASED THAN I.

AFTER TWO YEARS IN YERAVDA PRISON, GANDHI HAD TO UNDERGO AN OPERATION FOR APPENDICITIS, AFTER WHICH HE WAS RELEASED. THOUGH FREE, FOR THE REMAINING FOUR YEARS, GANDHI CARRIED ON NO ACTIVE AGITATION AGAINST THE GOVERNMENT. INSTEAD, HE DEVOTED HIS TIME TO SPREADING KHADI AND THE REMOVAL OF UNTOUCHABILITY.

THEN IN FEBRUARY 1928, THE SIMON COMMISSION, APPOINTED BY THE BRITISH GOVERNMENT, CAME TO INDIA TO SEE WHAT FURTHER POLITICAL REFORMS MIGHT BE GRANTED. THERE WAS NO INDIAN ON THE COMMISSION. ALL PARTIES IN THE COUNTRY BOYCOTTED IT. WHEREVER IT WENT —

PATRIOTS WHO TOOK OUT PROCESSIONS OF PROTEST WERE BEATEN MERCILESSLY. IN LAHORE, LALA LAJPATRAI WAS WOUNDED BY THE POLICE DURING A BOYCOTT PROCESSION. HE DIED A FEW DAYS LATER.

MEANWHILE IN BARDOLI, GUJARAT, PEASANTS ROSE IN REVOLT AGAINST THE UNJUST INCREASE IN LAND TAXES LEVIED BY THE GOVERNMENT. LED BY VALLABHBHAI PATEL, THEY REFUSED TO PAY THE TAXES.

GANDHI, THEN AT AHMEDABAD, SUPPORTED THE PEOPLE'S DEMAND AND INSPIRED THEM WITH COURAGE.

TO BREAK THEIR SPIRIT, THE GOVERNMENT CONFISCATED THEIR LANDS, HOUSEHOLD GOODS AND EVEN THEIR BUFFALOES.

LET THEM TAKE OUR BULLOCKS, OUR UTENSILS, OR WHATEVER THEY WANT.

WE WILL STARVE, BUT NOT PAY THE REVENUE.

THE PEACEFUL SATYAGRAHA WAS A VICTORY AGAINST THE GOVERNMENT'S AUTOCRACY. THE GOVERNMENT APPOINTED AN INQUIRY COMMITTEE WHICH UPHELD THE CASE OF THE PEASANTS OF BARDOLI. THE ENTIRE NATION WAS INSPIRED BY THE SUCCESS OF BARDOLI AND THE EXPERIMENT OF SATYAGRAHA. IT NOW PREPARED FOR THE GREATER BATTLE OF SWARAJ, WITH THE SAME WEAPON OF NON-VIOLENT SATYAGRAHA THAT BARDOLI HAD USED...

... AND AT THE STROKE OF MIDNIGHT ON DECEMBER 31, 1929, THE INDIAN NATIONAL CONGRESS, WITH JAWAHARLAL NEHRU PRESIDING, DECLARED COMPLETE INDEPENDENCE, OR POORNA SWARAJ, AS THE GOAL OF INDIA. IN ORDER TO ATTAIN IT...

... TO LAUNCH UPON A PROGRAMME OF CIVIL DIS-OBEDIENCE, INCLUDING NON-PAYMENT OF TAXES...

THE ALL-INDIA CONGRESS COMMITTEE HAD BEEN AUTHORISED TO PLAN AND CARRY OUT THE PROGRAMME, BUT THE REAL DECISION LAY WITH GANDHI.

AND GANDHI, AS A FIRST STEP IN THE COMING BATTLE, ASKED THE PEOPLE TO TAKE THE PLEDGE OF INDEPENDENCE ON JANUARY 26, 1930.*

WE BELIEVE THAT IT IS THE RIGHT OF THE INDIAN PEOPLE, AS OF ANY OTHER PEOPLE, TO HAVE FREEDOM AND TO ENJOY THE FRUITS OF THEIR TOIL.

THE BRITISH GOVERNMENT HAS RUINED INDIA ECONOMICALLY, POLITICALLY, CULTURALLY AND SPIRITUALLY... WE HOLD IT TO BE A CRIME AGAINST MAN AND GOD TO SUBMIT ANY LONGER TO A RULE THAT HAS CAUSED THIS FOUR-FOLD DISASTER TO OUR COUNTRY.

MANY CAME FORWARD TO TAKE THE PLEDGE.

GANDHI TOOK MORE THAN TWO MONTHS TO DECIDE HOW TO START THE BATTLE. THEN, HAVING MADE UP HIS MIND, HE WROTE TO THE VICEROY LORD IRWIN ON MARCH 2.

...THE BRITISH SYSTEM SEEMS TO BE DESIGNED TO CRUSH THE VERY LIFE OUT OF THE PEASANT. EVEN THE SALT HE MUST USE TO LIVE, IS SO TAXED AS TO MAKE THE BURDEN FALL HEAVIEST ON HIM THE BRITISH ADMINISTRATION IS THE MOST EXPENSIVE IN THE WORLD. TAKE YOUR OWN SALARY...IT IS OVER RS. 21,000 PER MONTH. THE BRITISH PRIME MINISTER GETS OVER RS. 5,400 PER MONTH...

...IF INDIA IS TO LIVE AS A NATION, THE SLOW DEATH BY STARVATION OF HER PEOPLE IS TO STOP, SOME REMEDY MUST BE FOUND. IF MY LETTER MAKES NO APPEAL TO YOUR HEART, I SHALL PROCEED WITH SUCH CO-WORKERS OF THE ASHRAM I CAN TAKE, TO DISREGARD THE PROVISIONS OF THE SALT LAWS.

GANDHI'S LETTER DID NOT APPEAL TO THE VICEROY'S HEART. AND SO CAME THE MEMORABLE DAY IN THE HISTORY OF MODERN INDIA. 12 TH MARCH 1930. AT 6.30 IN THE MORNING AT THE ASHRAM, GANDHI ADDRESSED HIS BAND OF SEVENTY-EIGHT SATYAGRAHIS. WHAT THEY WERE ABOUT TO LAUNCH WAS THE FINAL STRUGGLE.

WE HOPE TO BECOME THE REPRESENTATIVES OF THE POOREST OF THE POOR, THE LOWLIEST OF THE LOW, AND WEAKEST OF THE WEAK.

*TWENTY YEARS LATER, IN 1950, THE INDEPENDENCE DAY OF 1930 BECAME THE REPUBLIC DAY OF FREE INDIA.

AS THE SIXTYONE-YEAR-OLD GANDHI STEPPED OUT OF THE ASHRAM, A GREAT SHIVER OF EXCITEMENT RAN THROUGH THE CROWD.

WROTE THE "BOMBAY CHRONICLE":

THE SCENES THAT PRECEDED, ACCOMPANIED AND FOLLOWED THIS NATIONAL EVENT WERE SO MAGNIFICENT AND SOUL-STIRRING THAT THEY BEGGAR DESCRIPTION.

SAID JAWAHARLAL NEHRU:

TODAY THE PILGRIM MARCHES ONWARD ON HIS LONG TREK. STAFF IN HAND, HE GOES...CLEAR-EYED AND FIRM OF STEP, THE FIRE OF A GREAT RESOLVE IS IN HIM AND SURPASSING LOVE OF HIS MISERABLE COUNTRY-MEN.

THOUSANDS GATHERED TO WELCOME THE MAHATMA AT EVERY VILLAGE ON THE ROUTE. TO ALL OF THEM GANDHI SAID THE SAME THING—

SPIN EVERY DAY AND WEAR KHADI. ABOLISH UNTOUCHABILITY BANISH THE EVIL OF DRINK.

WALKING A DISTANCE OF THREE HUNDRED AND EIGHTY FIVE KM IN TWENTY-FOUR DAYS, GANDHI AND HIS SATYA-GRAHIS ARRIVED AT DANDI ON THE SEACOAST OF SOUTH GUJARAT ON THE MORNING OF 5TH APRIL*.

THE NEXT DAY —

HAIL, DELIVERER!

*6TH APRIL TO 13TH APRIL WAS OBSERVED AS NATIONAL WEEK IN MEMORY OF THE EVENTS LEADING TO THE JALLIANWALLA BAGH EPISODE IN 1919.

ALL INDIA WAS EXCITED. THE MAKING OF ILLEGAL SALT BECAME A WAY OF PROTEST ALONG THE SEACOAST. INDIANS BEGAN TO MAKE AND SELL SALT.

THE GOVERNMENT, ALARMED BY THIS FEARLESS DEFIANCE, TRIED TO STOP THE MOVEMENT USING HARSH METHODS.

THE WOMEN OF GUJARAT, FIRED BY THE SPIRIT OF PATRIOTISM, WANTED TO JOIN GANDHI'S BATTLE OF SATYAGRAHA. GANDHI TOLD THEM —

THE IMPATIENCE OF SOME SISTERS TO JOIN THE FIGHT IS A HEALTHY SIGN. IN THIS NON-VIOLENT WARFARE, THEIR CONTRIBUTION SHOULD BE MUCH GREATER THAN MEN'S.

TO CALL THE WOMAN THE WEAKER SEX IS A LIBEL; IT IS MAN'S INJUSTICE TO WOMAN. IF BY STRENGTH IS MEANT MORAL POWER, THEN WOMAN IS IMMEASURABLY MAN'S SUPERIOR.

AND THUS GANDHI ENCOURAGED THE WOMEN TO PARTICIPATE IN THE SATYAGRAHA MOVEMENT.

PLEASE DO NOT BUY FOREIGN CLOTH.

DO NOT INDULGE IN DRINKING. PLEASE GO BACK.

AND THOUSANDS OF WOMEN IN THE COUNTRY STEPPED OUT FROM THE CONFINES OF THEIR HOMES TO TAKE UP PUBLIC WORK AND PUBLIC SERVICE.

GANDHI TERMED THE POLICE BRUTALITIES THAT FOLLOWED THE DANDI MARCH AS "GOONDA RAAJ." ON MAY 3, HE WROTE TO THE VICEROY OF HIS INTENTION TO RAID THE GOVERNMENT SALT WORKS AT DHARASANA.* HE WAS ARRESTED THE VERY NEXT DAY...

...AND THE SATYAGRAHI RAID WAS LED BY SAROJINI NAIDU. ON THE MORNING OF MAY 21, A DISCIPLINED ARMY OF 2,500 SATYAGRAHI HEROES GOT READY FOR THE ATTACK. AFTER PRAYERS —

GANDHI'S BODY IS IN JAIL. BUT HIS SOUL IS WITH YOU. INDIA'S PRESTIGE IS IN YOUR HANDS. YOU MUST NOT USE ANY VIOLENCE. YOU WILL BE BEATEN. BUT YOU MUST NOT RESIST. YOU MUST NOT EVEN RAISE A HAND TO WARD OFF BLOWS.

THE SATYAGRAHI RAID BEGAN. THE FIRST BATCH OF VOLUNTEERS MOVED FORWARD.

* A FEW MILES TO THE NORTH OF DANDI.

AAAAH!

AAAAH!

KILL THOSE BRUTAL POLICEMEN!

BE CALM. THIS IS THE PRICE OF SATYAGRAHA.

THE NEXT LINE OF BRAVE MEN MOVED FORWARD.

IN THE COURSE OF THE DAY, SOME 700 SATYA-GRAHIS WERE BEATEN UP.

THE DHARASANA RAIDS SOON STOPPED, BUT THE SALT SATYAGRAHA CONTINUED. GRADUALLY BRITISH PUBLIC OPINION UNDERWENT A CHANGE. GANDHI WAS RELEASED ON INDEPENDENCE DAY— JANUARY 26, 1931. HE WAS INVITED FOR TALKS BY LORD IRWIN AT THE VICEREGAL PALACE ON FEBRUARY 17.

MANY ENGLISHMEN, INCLUDING CHURCHILL, WERE AGAINST THE IDEA OF "A HALF-NAKED FAKIR" BEING TREATED BY THE VICEROY. BUT LORD IRWIN WAS FRIENDLY. WHEN TEA WAS SERVED —

THANK YOU. I WILL ADD SOME SALT TO IT TO REMIND US OF THE FAMOUS BOSTON TEA PARTY.*

* IN 1773 THE AMERICANS HAD THROWN ENGLISH TEA BOXES INTO THE SEA AT BOSTON HARBOUR IN PROTEST AGAINST THE TAX ON TEA.

AND DURING THE TALKS THE NEXT DAY —

MR. GANDHI, YOU PLANNED A FINE STRATEGY ROUND THE ISSUE OF SALT.

THE TWO LEADERS SIGNED THE GANDHI-IRWIN PACT. GANDHI, ON BEHALF OF THE CONGRESS, AGREED TO STOP CIVIL DISOBEDIENCE, AND THE VICEROY AGREED TO RELEASE THE SATYAGRAHI PRISONERS, TO PERMIT PEACEFUL PICKETING OF FOREIGN CLOTH SHOPS AND LIQUOR BOOTHS, TO RETURN GOODS AND LANDS CONFISCATED FOR NON-PAYMENT OF LAND REVENUE AND TO PERMIT MAKING OF SALT ON SEA-COASTS BY LOCAL RESIDENTS FOR THEIR PRIVATE USE.

AS DECIDED IN THE PACT, GANDHI ATTENDED THE SECOND ROUND TABLE CONFERENCE TO DECIDE INDIA'S FUTURE. HE ARRIVED IN ENGLAND IN SEPTEMBER 1931 BY THE S.S. RAJPUTANA. HE STAYED AS A GUEST IN KINGSLEY HALL, A SETTLEMENT OF CHILDREN IN THE POOR EAST END QUARTER OF LONDON. AS HE TOOK HIS MORNING WALKS —

HELLO, UNCLE GANDHI!

HEY, GANDHI! WHERE'RE YOUR TROUSERS?

HA, HA, HA!

THE CONFERENCE FAILED. THE INDIAN DELEGATES HAD BEEN CAREFULLY SELECTED BY THE VICEROY TO REPRESENT VARIOUS GROUPS AND INTERESTS, NOT INDIA AS A WHOLE.

THEY REPRESENTED INDIA AS A HOUSE DIVIDED AGAINST ITSELF.

IN CONTRAST —

THE CONGRESS REPRESENTS NO PARTICULAR COMMUNITY, NO PARTICULAR INTEREST. IT CLAIMS TO REPRESENT ALL INDIAN INTERESTS AND ALL CLASSES. ABOVE ALL, THE DUMB, SEMI-STARVED MILLIONS IN 7,00,000 VILLAGES...

DURING THIS VISIT, GANDHI MET A LARGE NUMBER OF ENGLISHMEN, IN PUBLIC LIFE, AND PROFESSORS AT THE UNIVERSITIES OF OXFORD AND CAMBRIDGE AND GAINED THE LOVE AND RESPECT OF ALL.

...OF ALL INDIANS, YOU ARE THE ONE THAT THE REAL ENGLISHMAN LIKES AND UNDER-STANDS.

NO MATTER WHAT BEFALLS ME, ONE THING I SHALL CERTAINLY CARRY WITH ME, THAT IS THAT FROM HIGH TO LOW, I HAVE FOUND NOTHING BUT THE UTMOST COURTESY AND THE UTMOST AFFECTION. IT HAS DEEPENED MY FAITH IN HUMAN NATURE.

BUT BACK IN INDIA, THE VICEROY, LORD WILLINGDON, AND THE BRITISH OFFICIALS WERE NOT FRIENDLY. ALARMED BY THE SPREADING UNREST IN THE U.P., THE FRONTIER PROVINCE AND BENGAL, THE VICEROY DECIDED TO CRUSH THE CONGRESS. JAWAHARLAL NEHRU AND KHAN ABDUL GHAFFAR KHAN WERE ARRESTED...

...AND PROCLAIMED REPRESSIVE ORDINANCES IN THE THREE PROVINCES.

GANDHI LANDED IN BOMBAY ON THE MORNING OF DECEMBER 28, 1931, AND IN THE EVENING, ADDRESSED A HUGE MASS MEETING ON THE AZAD MAIDAN.

LAST YEAR WE FACED LATHIS, BUT THIS TIME WE MUST BE PREPARED TO FACE BULLETS... IF THERE IS TO BE A FIGHT, BE PREPARED FOR EVERY SACRIFICE.

GANDHI REQUESTED AN INTERVIEW WITH THE VICEROY TO DISCUSS HOW THE STATE OF PEACE BETWEEN THE GOVERNMENT AND THE CONGRESS COULD BE CONTINUED. THE VICEROY ARROGANTLY REFUSED THE REQUEST AND, INSTEAD, ARRESTED GANDHI ON JANUARY 4, 1932. AND SO THE SATYAGRAHA STARTED AGAIN AND THOUSANDS WERE JAILED IN A FEW MONTHS INCLUDING ALL CONGRESS LEADERS.

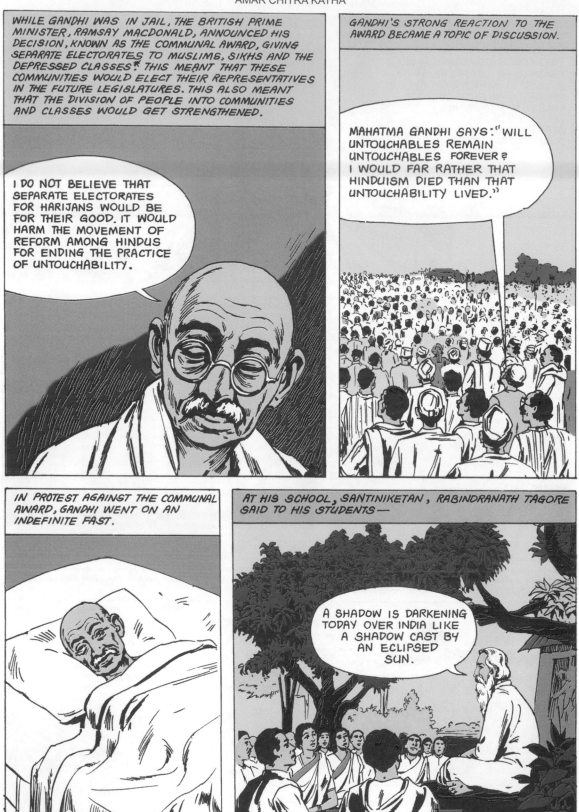

WHILE GANDHI WAS IN JAIL, THE BRITISH PRIME MINISTER, RAMSAY MACDONALD, ANNOUNCED HIS DECISION, KNOWN AS THE COMMUNAL AWARD, GIVING SEPARATE ELECTORATES TO MUSLIMS, SIKHS AND THE DEPRESSED CLASSES.* THIS MEANT THAT THESE COMMUNITIES WOULD ELECT THEIR REPRESENTATIVES IN THE FUTURE LEGISLATURES. THIS ALSO MEANT THAT THE DIVISION OF PEOPLE INTO COMMUNITIES AND CLASSES WOULD GET STRENGTHENED.

I DO NOT BELIEVE THAT SEPARATE ELECTORATES FOR HARIJANS WOULD BE FOR THEIR GOOD. IT WOULD HARM THE MOVEMENT OF REFORM AMONG HINDUS FOR ENDING THE PRACTICE OF UNTOUCHABILITY.

GANDHI'S STRONG REACTION TO THE AWARD BECAME A TOPIC OF DISCUSSION.

MAHATMA GANDHI SAYS:" WILL UNTOUCHABLES REMAIN UNTOUCHABLES FOREVER? I WOULD FAR RATHER THAT HINDUISM DIED THAN THAT UNTOUCHABILITY LIVED."

IN PROTEST AGAINST THE COMMUNAL AWARD, GANDHI WENT ON AN INDEFINITE FAST.

AT HIS SCHOOL, SANTINIKETAN, RABINDRANATH TAGORE SAID TO HIS STUDENTS—

A SHADOW IS DARKENING TODAY OVER INDIA LIKE A SHADOW CAST BY AN ECLIPSED SUN.

* THE 'UNTOUCHABLES'.

AND IT HAPPENED. THERE WAS A GREAT WAVE OF AWAKENING AGAINST UNTOUCHABILITY THROUGH-OUT THE COUNTRY. SOME WELL-KNOWN TEMPLES OPENED THEIR DOORS TO HARIJANS, AND ENTHUSIASTIC REFORMERS ARRANGED JOINT DINNERS OF CASTE HINDUS AND HARIJANS.

FOR GANDHI, WHOSE CONDITION WAS BY NOW CRITICAL, IT WAS "A MODERN MIRACLE". TO THE NATIONAL LEADERS HE CONVEYED HIS DECISION TO FAST UNTO DEATH, UNLESS THE COMMUNAL AWARD WAS REVOKED.

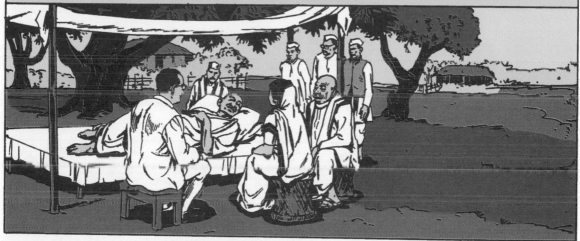

THE SETTLEMENT MADE IN YERAVDA JAIL WAS DISCUSSED AND APPROVED AT THE CONFERENCE OF HINDU LEADERS IN BOMBAY, IN SEPTEMBER.

...NO ONE SHALL BE REGARDED AS AN UNTOUCHABLE BY REASON OF HIS BIRTH, AND THOSE WHO HAVE BEEN SO REGARDED HITHERTO, WILL HAVE THE SAME RIGHTS AS THE OTHER HINDUS IN REGARD TO THE USE OF PUBLIC WELLS, PUBLIC ROADS AND OTHER PUBLIC INSTITUTIONS. THIS RIGHT SHALL BE ONE OF THE EARLIEST ACTS OF THE SWARAJ PARLIAMENT...

AFTER FOUR DAYS OF NEGOTIATIONS BETWEEN THE LEADERS AND DR. B.R. AMBEDKAR, A SETTLEMENT WAS REACHED ON SEPTEMBER 25 AND THE PRIME MINISTER INFORMED OF IT. WHEN THE BRITISH GOVERNMENT ACCEPTED THE TERMS OF THE POONA PACT, GANDHI BROKE HIS FAST ON THE AFTERNOON OF SEPTEMBER 26, 1932.

DURING THE NEGOTIATIONS, GANDHI HAD OFFERED DR. AMBEDKAR MORE THAN HE HAD AGREED TO ACCEPT FROM THE HINDU LEADERS. DR. AMBEDKAR PRAISED GANDHI FOR THIS AT A PUBLIC MEETING HELD IN BOMBAY ON THE SAME DAY.

I WAS IMMENSELY SURPRISED WHEN I MET HIM. THAT THERE WAS SO MUCH IN COMMON BETWEEN HIM AND ME... WHENEVER ANY DISPUTES WERE CARRIED TO HIM... HE CAME IMMEDIATELY TO MY RESCUE AND NOT TO THE RESCUE OF THE OTHER SIDE. I AM VERY GRATEFUL TO MAHATMAJI...

FOR GANDHI THE POONA PACT WAS ONLY A BEGINNING. EVEN WHILE IN JAIL, HE ISSUED STATEMENTS, LETTERS AND MESSAGES TO GUIDE PEOPLE IN REMOVING UNTOUCHABILITY IN ALL WALKS OF LIFE.

HE FORMED THE HARIJAN SEVAK SANGH, AND STARTED THREE WEEKLIES TO PROPAGATE THE MESSAGE OF ANTI-UNTOUCHABILITY: THE 'HARIJAN' IN ENGLISH, THE 'HARIJAN SEVAK' IN HINDI, AND THE 'HARIJAN BANDHU' IN GUJARATI.

THOUGH HE WAS RELEASED ON MAY 8, 1933, HE SERVED TWO MORE TERMS IN PRISON AND WAS FINALLY RELEASED IN AUGUST 1933. HE UNDERTOOK A NINE MONTHS' TOUR OF THE COUNTRY, FROM NOVEMBER 1933 TO JUNE 1934, COVERING NEARLY 20,000 KM AND COLLECTED 8 LAKHS FOR HARIJAN UPLIFTMENT WORK AND FOR THE PROPAGATION OF HIS MESSAGE OF ABOLITION OF UNTOUCHABILITY.

AT ONE PLACE IN BIHAR, HIS CAR WAS ATTACKED ON THE HOOD WITH A LATHI BY THE ORTHODOX, AND A STONE HIT THE GLASS BEHIND THE SEAT. AND IN PUNE, ON JUNE 25, 1934, A BOMB WAS THROWN AT ONE OF THE CARS CARRYING HIM TO A PUBLIC MEETING.

WROTE GANDHI IN 'HARIJAN'—

I HAVE NOTHING BUT DEEP PITY FOR THE UNKNOWN THROWER OF THE BOMB... LET THE REFORMERS NOT BE INCENSED AGAINST THE BOMB-THROWER OR THOSE WHO MAY BE BEHIND HIM.

AFTER THE TOUR, GANDHI RETIRED FROM ACTIVE POLITICS, GUIDING THE CONGRESS FROM OUTSIDE. HE WAS DEEPLY TROUBLED BY THE POVERTY OF THE VILLAGES WHICH HE HAD SEEN DURING THE TOUR, AND GOT THE CONGRESS TO ESTABLISH THE ALL-INDIA VILLAGE INDUSTRIES ASSOCIATION TO REVIVE THE DYING VILLAGE INDUSTRIES.

GANDHI'S AIM IN STARTING THE VILLAGE CRAFTS PROGRAMMES WAS NOT ONLY ECONOMICAL, BUT ALSO MORAL. CENTURIES OF OPPRESSION AND POVERTY HAD BROKEN THE SPIRIT OF THE VILLAGE CRAFTSMEN.

HE BUILT A SMALL COTTAGE FOR HIMSELF AT SEGAON.* HELPING HIM IN THIS REVIVAL OF VILLAGE INDUSTRIES WAS MIRABEHN, AN ENGLISHWOMAN WHO, INSPIRED BY GANDHI'S WORK, HAD COME IN 1925 ALL THE WAY FROM ENGLAND.

THE COTTAGE GREW INTO A KIND OF RURAL ASHRAM. PEOPLE WHO WANTED TO MEET GANDHI TO DISCUSS ANYTHING WITH HIM GATHERED THERE.

AS THE SALT SATYAGRAHA OF 1930 HAD DRAWN ATTENTION TO THE INJUSTICE OF BRITISH RULE, SO THIS ASHRAM IN THE HEART OF RURAL INDIA, DREW THE ATTENTION OF THE COUNTRY'S LEADERS AND OF THE CITY PEOPLE TO THE CONDITION OF VILLAGES.

AS AN OUTCOME OF THE ROUND TABLE CONFERENCES, THE GOVERNMENT OF INDIA ACT 1935 WAS PASSED GRANTING PARTIAL AUTONOMY TO THE PROVINCES. THE CONGRESS WON HANDSOMELY IN THE ELECTIONS HELD IN 1937, FORMING MINISTRIES IN EIGHT OUT OF THE ELEVEN PROVINCES IN THE COUNTRY.†

THE MUSLIM LEAGUE, HEADED BY M.A. JINNAH, DID POORLY AT THE ELECTIONS AND GOT NO SHARE OF POWER IN ANY OF THE PROVINCES. ANGRY, JINNAH STARTED A CAMPAIGN AMONG THE MUSLIMS WITH THE CRY, "ISLAM IN DANGER".

CONGRESS PRESIDENT, SUBHAS CHANDRA BOSE, MET JINNAH AT HIS RESIDENCE IN BOMBAY, TO DISCUSS HIS DEMANDS, BUT THEY COULD NOT COME TO AN UNDERSTANDING.

JINNAH'S CAMPAIGN SUCCEEDED SO WELL THAT IN TWO OR THREE YEARS, HE BECAME THE MOST POWERFUL MUSLIM LEADER.

* A VILLAGE LATER NAMED SEVAGRAM, ABOUT TEN KM FROM WARDHA IN MAHARASHTRA.
† IN ALL PROVINCES EXCEPT BENGAL, THE PUNJAB AND SIND.

THEN IN SEPTEMBER 1939 WORLD WAR II BROKE. THE THREAT OF HITLER LOOMED OVER ENGLAND AND FRANCE.

THE CONGRESS ASKED FOR THE PROMISE OF FREEDOM AFTER THE WAR IN RETURN FOR HELP IN THE WAR EFFORT.

WHEN THE BRITISH GOVERMENT REFUSED, THE CONGRESS MINISTRIES RESIGNED. JINNAH CALLED ON THE MUSLIMS TO CELEBRATE DECEMBER 22, 1939 AS "DELIVERANCE DAY"* HE PERSUADED THE MUSLIM LEAGUE SESSION AT LAHORE ON MARCH 24, 1940, TO DEMAND THE PARTITION OF INDIA AND THE FORMATION OF A MUSLIM STATE, PAKISTAN.

JINNAH TERMED THE HINDUS AND THE MUSLIMS 'TWO NATIONS'.

GANDHI WAS DEEPLY PAINED BY JINNAH'S STATEMENT.

THE "TWO-NATIONS" THEORY IS AN UNTRUTH. AS A MAN OF NON-VIOLENCE, I CANNOT FORCIBLY RESIST THE PROPOSED PARTITION IF THE MUSLIMS OF INDIA INSIST UPON IT. BUT I CAN NEVER BE A WILLING PARTY TO THE VIVISECTION...

FOR IT MEANS THE UNDOING OF CENTURIES OF WORK DONE BY NUMBER- LESS HINDUS AND MUSLIMS TO LIVE TOGETHER AS ONE NATION. MY WHOLE SOUL REBELS AGAINST THE IDEA THAT HINDUISM AND ISLAM REPRESENT TWO ANTAGONISTIC CULTURES AND DOCTRINES.

* DAY OF DELIVERANCE FROM THE CONGRESS RULE.

IN JUNE 1940, CHURCHILL BECAME THE PRIME MINISTER OF GREAT BRITAIN AND THE HOPE OF THE CONGRESS DEMANDS BEING MET BY THE BRITISH GOVERNMENT DWINDLED. MASS CIVIL DISOBEDIENCE WAS NOW REPLACED BY INDIVIDUAL SATYAGRAHA. ONE BY ONE SENIOR CONGRESS LEADERS AND PEOPLE WEDDED TO THE GANDHIAN WAY OF LIFE INCLUDING VINOBA BHAVE, JAWAHARLAL NEHRU, VALLABHBHAI PATEL, ABUL KALAM AZAD, WERE PICKED BY GANDHI AS SATYAGRAHIS. THEY GAVE ANTI-WAR SPEECHES AND WERE PROMPTLY ARRESTED AND JAILED.

AFTER THE LEADERS FOLLOWED AN UNENDING STREAM OF ORDINARY CONGRESS WORKERS COURTING IMPRISONMENT.

THERE WAS TO BE NO MASS EXCITEMENT AND NO MASS DEMONSTRATION, AS IN 1930, AND NO OBSTRUCTION TO THE WORK OF THE GOVERNMENT.

IN JUNE 1941, HITLER INVADED THE SOVIET UNION AND IN DECEMBER, JAPAN JOINED THE AXIS POWERS, GERMANY AND ITALY. THE WAR BECAME REALLY GLOBAL NOW.

BY MARCH 1942, THE JAPANESE WERE IN BURMA AND WERE MOVING TOWARDS INDIA.

IN DECEMBER 1941, INDIVIDUAL SATYAGRAHIS WERE RELEASED FROM JAIL. ON MARCH 23, 1942 SIR STAFFORD CRIPPS, A MEMBER OF THE BRITISH CABINET, ARRIVED WITH A NEW OFFER.

IT PROMISED FREEMDOM AFTER THE WAR, AND A CONSTITUTION FORMED BY INDIANS. BUT IT ALSO GAVE PROVINCES AND PRINCES THE OPTION TO KEEP OUT OF THE NEW GOVERNMENT.

THIS COULD LEAD NOT ONLY TO TWO INDIAS ,, BUT SEVERAL OF THEM. DESCRIBING THE PROPOSALS AS A POST-DATED CHEQUE, GANDHI WAS RATHER BLUNT DURING HIS MEETING WITH CRIPPS.

WHY DID YOU COME IF THIS IS WHAT YOU HAVE TO OFFER? I WOULD ADVISE YOU TO TAKE THE NEXT PLANE HOME.

THE CONGRESS WORKING COMMITTEE ALSO REJECTED THE OFFER WHICH LEFT INDIANS WITH NO POWER TO FIGHT THE JAPANESE IN THE EVENT OF AN ATTACK. MEANWHILE, SUBHAS CHANDRA BOSE WHO HAD REACHED JAPAN IN JANUARY 1941, URGED THE PEOPLE THROUGH RADIO MESSAGES TO FIGHT THE BRITISH WITH THE HELP OF THE JAPANESE.

GANDHI URGED THE BRITISH TO HAND OVER CONTROL TO A NATIONAL GOVERNMENT WHICH WOULD CO-OPERATE WITH THE BRITISH AND AMERICAN ARMIES TO DEFEND INDIA AGAINST THE JAPANESE.

GANDHI'S STAND WAS SUPPORTED BY THE MEETING OF THE ALL-INDIA CONGRESS COMMITTEE IN AUGUST 1942. AT A MEETING AT GAWALIA TANK, THE 'QUIT INDIA' RESOLUTION WAS PASSED.

... THE IMMEDIATE ENDING OF BRITISH RULE IN INDIA IS AN URGENT NECESSITY. BOTH FOR THE SAKE OF INDIA AND FOR THE SUCCESS OF THE CAUSE OF THE UNITED NATIONS.* THE COMMITTEE, THEREFORE, RESOLVES TO SANCTION THE STARTING OF A MASS STRUGGLE ON NON-VIOLENT LINES ON THE WIDEST POSSIBLE SCALE, UNDER THE LEADERSHIP OF GANDHIJI.

GANDHI HAD TOLD THE A.I.C.C ON AUGUST 7 —

AT A TIME WHEN I AM ABOUT TO LAUNCH THE BIGGEST FIGHT IN MY LIFE, THERE CAN BE NO HATRED FOR THE BRITISH IN MY HEART. IN A MOMENT OF ANGER, THEY MIGHT DO THINGS WHICH MIGHT PROVOKE YOU. NEVER-THELESS, YOU SHOULD NOT RESORT TO VIOLENCE ...

THE GOVERNMENT DID, IN ANGER, ACT RASHLY. THOUGH GANDHI HAD DECLARED THAT HE WOULD NOT START THE MOVEMENT BEFORE HE HAD SEEN THE VICEROY...

... THE GOVERNMENT ARRESTED GANDHI AND ALL MEMBERS OF THE WORKING COMMITTEE EARLY IN THE MORNING OF AUGUST 9. BEFORE BEING TAKEN AWAY BY THE POLICE, GANDHI GAVE A MESSAGE TO "EVERY NON-VIOLENT SOLDIER OF FREEDOM".

DO OR DIE.

* ENGLAND, FRANCE AND AMERICA.

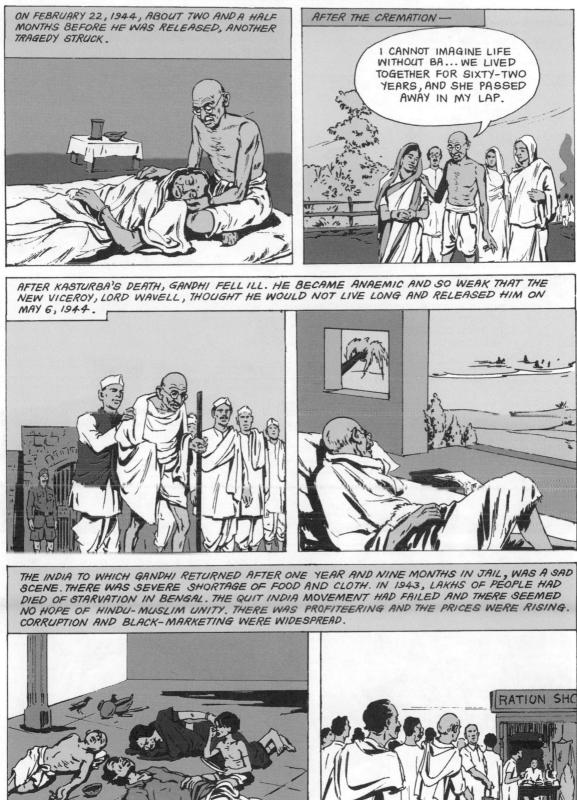

ON FEBRUARY 22, 1944, ABOUT TWO AND A HALF MONTHS BEFORE HE WAS RELEASED, ANOTHER TRAGEDY STRUCK.

AFTER THE CREMATION—

I CANNOT IMAGINE LIFE WITHOUT BA... WE LIVED TOGETHER FOR SIXTY-TWO YEARS, AND SHE PASSED AWAY IN MY LAP.

AFTER KASTURBA'S DEATH, GANDHI FELL ILL. HE BECAME ANAEMIC AND SO WEAK THAT THE NEW VICEROY, LORD WAVELL, THOUGHT HE WOULD NOT LIVE LONG AND RELEASED HIM ON MAY 6, 1944.

THE INDIA TO WHICH GANDHI RETURNED AFTER ONE YEAR AND NINE MONTHS IN JAIL, WAS A SAD SCENE. THERE WAS SEVERE SHORTAGE OF FOOD AND CLOTH. IN 1943, LAKHS OF PEOPLE HAD DIED OF STARVATION IN BENGAL. THE QUIT INDIA MOVEMENT HAD FAILED AND THERE SEEMED NO HOPE OF HINDU-MUSLIM UNITY. THERE WAS PROFITEERING AND THE PRICES WERE RISING. CORRUPTION AND BLACK-MARKETING WERE WIDESPREAD.

RATION SHO

GANDHI MET JINNAH AT HIS RESIDENCE IN BOMBAY DAY AFTER DAY FROM SEPTEMBER 9 TO 26, AND TRIED TO PERSUADE HIM TO GIVE UP HIS DEMAND FOR PAKISTAN. HE OFFERED JINNAH THE SUBSTANCE OF PAKISTAN WITHOUT PARTITION.

WHEN THE TALKS FAILED, GANDHI APPEALED TO THE PRESS AND PUBLIC TO AVOID PARTISAN-SHIP AND BITTERNESS.

GANDHI TOLD A CORRESPONDENT OF A LONDON NEWSPAPER—

WE HAVE PARTED AS FRIENDS. I AM CONVINCED THAT MR. JINNAH IS A GOOD MAN. I AM A MAN OF PRAYER AND I SHALL PRAY FOR UNDERSTANDING.

GANDHI NOW TURNED HIS ATTENTION TO THE GROWING CORRUPTION IN INDIA.

THE UNBEARABLE FORCES OF INJUSTICES EXPLOITATION AND FALSEHOOD, PREVAILING IN THIS COUNTRY AND THE WORLD, STIFLE ME. THERE IS NOTHING LEFT LIKE MORAL PUBLIC OPINION...

I CANNOT TOLERATE OUR PEOPLE BEHAVING THUS, AND COLLECTING VAST FORTUNES AT THE COST OF PEOPLE'S STARVATION ...I FEEL I MUST DO PENANCE BY FASTING. AS A SATYAGRAHI I CANNOT BE A SILENT SPECTATOR OF ALL THESE THINGS.

FRIENDS AND CO-WORKERS ARGUED WITH GANDHI TO GIVE UP THE IDEA. BEFORE HE COULD DECIDE, HIS HEALTH FAILED. HE FELT WEAK AND EXHAUSTED. RAJAGOPALA-CHARI ADVISED HIM A MONTH'S "FAST FROM WORK" IN PLACE OF "FAST FROM FOOD". GANDHI ACCEPTED THE SUGGESTION.

FROM DECEMBER 4 TO 31, HE CONCENTRATED ON THE WORK FOR KASTURBA MEMORIAL TRUST, KHADI, AND POPULARISATION OF HINDI.

FROM MAY 1945, THE POLITICAL SITUATION CHANGED. GERMANY SURRENDERED ON MAY 7 AND WAS FOLLOWED BY JAPAN ON AUGUST 10.

IN THE LAST WEEK OF AUGUST, SUBHAS CHANDRA BOSE WAS INJURED IN A PLANE CRASH AND DIED IN JAPAN.

IN ENGLAND, THE LABOUR PARTY WON THE ELECTION BY A HUGE MAJORITY AND BEGAN CONSULTATIONS WITH THE VICEROY FOR A SETTLEMENT OF THE INDIAN PROBLEM.

IN FEBRUARY 1946, THE INDIAN SAILORS OF THE ROYAL INDIAN NAVY MUTINIED IN BOMBAY, AND FOR A DAY OR TWO, THERE WAS ANARCHY IN THE CITY.

BY THIS TIME, THE BRITISH GOVERNMENT REALISED THAT IT WOULD NOT BE ABLE TO RULE INDIA FOR VERY LONG AND DECIDED THAT SOON POWER WILL HAVE TO BE HANDED OVER TO INDIANS AS EARLY AS POSSIBLE.

THREE MINISTERS OF THE BRITISH CABINET, LORD PETHICK-LAWRENCE, SIR STAFFORD CRIPPS, AND A.V. ALEXANDER CAME OUT TO INDIA IN MARCH 1946 TO DISCUSS WITH INDIAN LEADERS HOW THIS COULD BE DONE.

IN SPITE OF PROLONGED DISCUSSIONS, THEY FAILED TO BRING ABOUT AGREEMENT BETWEEN THE CONGRESS AND THE MUSLIM LEAGUE. THE VICEROY THEN INVITED JAWAHARLAL NEHRU TO FORM A PROVISIONAL NATIONAL GOVERNMENT UNDER HIM.

BEFORE DOING SO NEHRU MET JINNAH TO INVITE HIM TO JOIN OR SEND REPRESENTATIVES OF THE MUSLIM LEAGUE TO JOIN THE GOVERNMENT. JINNAH REFUSED...

...AND CALLED ON MUSLIMS TO OBSERVE "DIRECT ACTION DAY" ON AUGUST 16.

"DIRECT ACTION" TOOK A VIOLENT TURN.

FIVE THOUSAND PEOPLE WERE KILLED AND MORE THAN TEN THOUSAND WOUNDED IN FOUR OR FIVE DAYS OF RIOTING IN THE STREETS OF CALCUTTA. ANGRY HINDUS HIT BACK FROM THE SECOND DAY ONWARDS.

IN A VICIOUS CIRCLE THE VIOLENCE CONTINUED. THE MUSLIMS IN THE VILLAGES OF THE NOAKHALI DISTRICT* NOW TOOK REVENGE ON THE HINDUS. GANDHI, DEEPLY SHOCKED, WENT TO BENGAL AND TRAVELLED FROM VILLAGE TO VILLAGE, WITH A FEW COMPANIONS...

...VISITING THE WOMEN IN THEIR HOMES TO COMFORT THEM...

...AND ASKING THE MEN TO SHED FEAR.

AFTER FOUR MONTHS IN NOAKHALI, GANDHI WENT TO BIHAR, WHERE THE HINDUS HAD TAKEN REVENGE ON THE MUSLIMS FOR THE MISDEEDS OF THE MUSLIMS OF NOAKHALI.

THERE IS SUCH A FIRE RAGING IN ME THAT I WOULD KNOW NO PEACE TILL I HAVE FOUND A SOLUTION FOR ALL THIS.

IT WAS ALL THE MORE CRUEL TO GANDHI BECAUSE DURING THE LOOTING AND ARSON—

MAHATMA GANDHI KI JAI.

* NOW IN BANGLADESH.

THE PEACE, HOWEVER, PROVED SHORT LIVED. THE TROUBLE STARTED AGAIN ON THE NIGHT OF AUGUST 31. A CROWD OF ANGRY HINDUS ATTACKED THE HOUSE IN THE MUSLIM LOCALITY IN WHICH GANDHI WAS STAYING, SMASHED ITS GLASS WINDOW-PANES, BROKE OPEN THE DOORS, AND RUSHED IN.

THE POLICE ARRIVED AND DISPERSED THE CROWD WITH TEAR-GAS.

GANDHI DECIDED TO FAST. IN A STATEMENT ON SEPTEMBER 1, 1947 HE ANNOUNCED.—

WHAT MY WORD IN PERSON CANNOT DO, MY FAST MAY. I BEGIN FASTING FROM 8.15 P.M. TO END ONLY IF AND WHEN SANITY RETURNS TO CALCUTTA.

THE FAST HAD THE DESIRED EFFECT. HINDU AND MUSLIM LEADERS JOINED IN APPEALING TO GANDHI TO END THE FAST. ON THE AFTERNOON OF SEPTEMBER 4, A DEPUTATION OF PROMINENT CITIZENS OF CALCUTTA PROMISED TO GANDHI IN WRITING:

WE SHALL NEVER AGAIN ALLOW COMMUNAL STRIFE IN THE CITY, AND SHALL STRIVE UNTO DEATH TO PREVENT IT.

GANDHI ENDED HIS FAST. CALCUTTA THUS RETURNED TO SANITY AND THERE WAS PEACE IN THE WHOLE OF WEST BENGAL THEREAFTER.

BUT THE CONFLAGRATION WAS SPREADING FAST IN DELHI AND IN THE TWO PUNJABS, INDIAN AND PAKISTANI. JAWAHARLAL NEHRU HAD WIRED TO GANDHI ON SEPTEMBER 2 TO GO TO THE PUNJAB AS EARLY AS POSSIBLE. GANDHI REACHED DELHI ON SEPTEMBER 9, AND AT THE EVENING PRAYER MEETING ON SEPTEMBER 10 —

HAS THE CITY OF DELHI, WHICH ALWAYS APPEARED GAY, TURNED INTO A CITY OF THE DEAD?

DELHI WAS IN CHAOS. THOUSANDS OF HINDU AND SIKH REFUGEES HAD POURED INTO THE CITY FROM PAKISTAN. THEY HAD DRIVEN OUT THE MUSLIMS FROM THEIR HOMES AND OCCUPIED THEM. GANDHI VISITED THE CAMPS IN WHICH THE MUSLIMS HAD TAKEN SHELTER, AND THE EDUCATIONAL CENTRE OF JAMIA MILLIA, RUN BY THE STAUNCH NATIONALIST MUSLIM : ZAKIR HUSAIN.*

* WHO LATER BECAME PRESIDENT OF INDIA, 1967-1969.

LATER GANDHI SPOKE TO THE HINDUS AND SIKHS ABOUT THE PLIGHT OF THE MUSLIMS.

ALL THESE PEOPLE ARE LIKE MY OWN SONS, LIKE MY OWN BROTHERS. I REQUEST YOU NOT TO REGARD THE MUSLIMS AS YOUR ENEMIES. I HAVE SEEN THE TERRIBLE PLIGHT OF HINDUS AND SIKHS OF PAKISTAN. DO YOU THINK I AM NOT PAINED...?

YOUR BROTHER IS MY BROTHER, YOUR MOTHER IS MY MOTHER, AND I HAVE THE SAME ANGUISH IN MY HEART AS YOU HAVE. WHAT DID GURU NANAK TEACH? NANAK SAHEB TRIED TO BRING TOGETHER ALL RELIGIONS... HE MADE NO DISTINCTION BETWEEN THE HINDUS, THE MUSLIMS AND THE SIKHS.

HE SPOKE TO THE MUSLIMS—

... THE MUSLIMS SHOULD OPEN-HEARTEDLY DECLARE THAT THEY BELONG TO INDIA AND ARE LOYAL TO THE UNION. IT WOULD BE A NOBLE THING IF THE MUSLIMS, LIKE THE HINDUS OF BIHAR AND CALCUTTA, REPENT AND ADMIT THAT THEY HAVE DONE WRONG THINGS... TODAY... BECAUSE OF YOU... HINDUS ARE VERY MUCH ANNOYED WITH ME...

I SHALL NOT BE SURPRISED IF ONE DAY, I FALL A PREY TO THIS FURY.

GANDHI'S PRESENCE AND WORDS BROUGHT CALM TO DELHI, BUT THE CALM WAS ONLY ON THE SURFACE. THERE WAS SO MUCH HATRED AND FEAR OF ONE ANOTHER IN PAKISTAN AND INDIA THAT LAKHS AND LAKHS OF HINDUS AND SIKHS LEFT PAKISTAN FOR INDIA, AND MUSLIMS OF INDIA FOR PAKISTAN.

MANY REFUGEES OF THE THREE COMMUNITIES DRAGGED EACH OTHER OUT OF THE TRAINS IN WHICH THEY WERE TRAVELLING, AND KILLED ONE ANOTHER.

SO AS IN CALCUTTA, GANDHI WENT ON AN INDEFINITE FAST FROM JANUARY 13, 1948. ON JANUARY 18, THE HINDU AND SIKH LEADERS IN DELHI PROMISED HIM THAT THEY WOULD...

... PROTECT THE LIFE, PROPERTY AND FAITH OF MUSLIMS AND THAT THE INCIDENTS WHICH HAVE TAKEN PLACE IN DELHI WILL NOT HAPPEN AGAIN.

ONLY THEN DID GANDHI BREAK HIS FAST.

BUT GANDHI'S EFFORTS TO UNITE THE PEOPLE DID NOT PLEASE EVERYONE. AT 5.10 P.M ON JANUARY 30, 1948 —

HE RAMA!

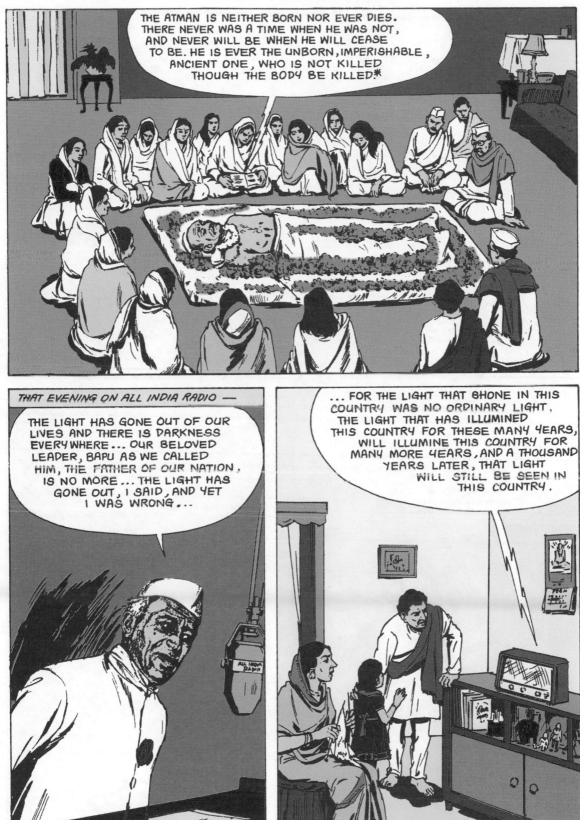

THE ATMAN IS NEITHER BORN NOR EVER DIES. THERE NEVER WAS A TIME WHEN HE WAS NOT, AND NEVER WILL BE WHEN HE WILL CEASE TO BE. HE IS EVER THE UNBORN, IMPERISHABLE, ANCIENT ONE, WHO IS NOT KILLED THOUGH THE BODY BE KILLED.✳

THAT EVENING ON ALL INDIA RADIO —

THE LIGHT HAS GONE OUT OF OUR LIVES AND THERE IS DARKNESS EVERYWHERE... OUR BELOVED LEADER, BAPU AS WE CALLED HIM, THE FATHER OF OUR NATION, IS NO MORE... THE LIGHT HAS GONE OUT, I SAID, AND YET I WAS WRONG...

...FOR THE LIGHT THAT SHONE IN THIS COUNTRY WAS NO ORDINARY LIGHT, THE LIGHT THAT HAS ILLUMINED THIS COUNTRY FOR THESE MANY YEARS, WILL ILLUMINE THIS COUNTRY FOR MANY MORE YEARS, AND A THOUSAND YEARS LATER, THAT LIGHT WILL STILL BE SEEN IN THIS COUNTRY.

✳ A VERSE FROM THE BHAGAVAD GITA.

ON FEBRUARY 2, 1948

A GLORY HAS DEPARTED, AND THE SUN THAT WARMED AND BRIGHTENED OUR LIVES HAS SET, AND WE SHIVER IN THE COLD AND DARK...THAT MAN WITH DIVINE FIRE CHARGED US ALSO ... OUT OF THAT DIVINE FIRE MANY OF US ALSO TOOK A SMALL SPARK WHICH STRENGTHENED... US...

... HE LIVES IN THE HEARTS OF MILLIONS, AND HE WILL LIVE FOR IMMEMORIAL AGES.

' **Non-violence is the greatest force at the disposal of mankind. It is mightier than the mightiest weapon of destruction devised by the ingenuity of man.** '

'When I despair, I remember that all through history the way of truth and love has always won. There have been tyrants and murderers and for a time they seem invincible but in the end, they always fall -- think of it, ALWAYS.'